BONHOEFFER'S HERITAGE

Also by Edwin Robertson

Paul Schneider: the Pastor of Buchenwald
Man's Estimate of Man
Tomorrow is a Holiday: A South American Journey
New Translations of the Bible
Take and Read: A Guide to Group Bible Study
Light in Darkness
Mini-Commentaries 8 & 9 (The Old Testament Prophets)
Corinthians One and Two
Local Broadcasting
Breakthrough
Chiara Lubich
Igino Giordani: The Flame of Love
The Wounded Healer (with Vera Phillips)
Wycliffe: Morning Star of the Reformation
Christians Against Hitler
*The Shame and the Sacrifice: The Life and Teaching of
   Dietrich Bonhoeffer*

BONHOEFFER'S HERITAGE

Edwin Robertson

Hodder & Stoughton

LONDON SYDNEY AUCKLAND TORONTO

British Library Cataloguing in Publication Data

Robertson, E. H. (Edwin Hornton), *1912*–
    Bonhoeffer's heritage.
    1. Christianity
    I. Title
    200

    ISBN 0-340-51477-9

CONTENTS

ACKNOWLEDGEMENTS

Many of the people to whom I am indebted for ideas and encouragement are mentioned in the course of this book. Primarily, of course, Eberhard Bethge, who first stimulated my imagination and gave me a starting-point in the chapter on 'Authentic Theology' in his *Bonhoeffer: Exile and Martyr*. There is also John Bowden, whose *Jesus: The Unanswered Questions* corresponded exactly with my own feeling about the necessity of questions in which I would meet the Jesus who was so question-able, and whose translation of Jacques Pohier's *God in Fragments* provided the substance of the Epilogue to Part Three.

There are others who read through parts of the text at a formative period in my writing and made comments which enabled me to proceed with confidence. These include the Ven. Francis House, the Rev. Keith Clements, David Wavre, as sympathetic publisher, and once again Eberhard Bethge.

I would like to pay tribute once again to the untiring work of Vera Phillips, who has wrestled with her word processor and patiently endured my many changes.

Edwin Robertson

INTRODUCTION

Among the many stimulating and disturbing letters that Dietrich Bonhoeffer wrote to his friend Eberhard Bethge was one sent to the Italian front, where Bethge was serving, on 3 August 1944.[1]

It came from Tegel Prison and urged Bethge to read again Bonhoeffer's long poem 'Night Voices in Tegel'.[2] There are very few poems which enable us to share the thoughts of men in prison more powerfully than that longest of Bonhoeffer's poems. It describes the environment in which he was working. But it also tells us of his sense of guilt, his involvement in the guilt. He broods and sinks himself 'into the depths of the dark', and calls upon the night:

> You night, full of outrage and evil,
> Make yourself known to me!
> Why and for how long will you try our patience?
> A deep and long silence;
> Then I hear the night bend down to me:
> 'I am not dark; only guilt is dark!'[3]

In the verses that follow he spells out the awful betrayal of humanity that he and so many Germans had witnessed:

> 'Our eyes had to see folly,
> In order to bind us in deep guilt;
> Then they stopped our mouths,
> And we were as dumb dogs.
>
> 'We learned to lie easily,
> To be at the disposal of open injustice;
> If the defenceless was abused,
> Then our eyes remained cold . . .

> 'The once holy bonds uniting men
> Were mangled and flayed,
> Friendship and faithfulness betrayed;
> Tears and rue were reviled.'[4]

And all this has been true of Germans, 'We sons of pious races,' whom he can remember as 'One-time defenders of right and truth.'[5] There is a long list of guilt and a prayer to fellow humans:

> 'Brother, till the night be past,
> Pray for me!'[6]

In the light of that poem and that deep sense of the darkness of guilt, Bonhoeffer refers to an 'Outline' for a book he wants to write:

> I'm enclosing the outline of a book that I've planned. I don't know whether you can get anything from it, but I think you more or less understand what I am driving at. I hope I shall be given the peace and strength to finish it. The church must come out of its stagnation. We must move out again into the open air of intellectual discussion with the world, and risk saying controversial things, if we are to get down to the serious problems of life.[7]

He was not given the 'peace and strength' to write the book. Bethge, however, carefully preserved Bonhoeffer's 'theological' letters, as he was instructed, and published them under the title, *Widerstand und Ergebung*. In English that is better known as *Letters and Papers from Prison*.[8]

To some extent, the letters and papers contain part of the book he intended to write. But there is more. The letters contain the beginning of the ideas; their explosive power was shown when John Robinson bound them up with Bultmann and Tillich to produce *Honest to God*.[9] Bonhoeffer would not have written *Honest to God*. He wanted, he said, to write a book of not more than a hundred pages, divided into three parts:

1 The Stocktaking of Christianity;
2 The Real Meaning of Christian Faith;
3 Conclusions.

And he proceeded to outline in some detail the contents of each of the three chapters.[10] That was in 1944. Had he lived, his outline would have grown into a much larger book as the experience of post-war Europe added material.

Many have been stimulated by Bonhoeffer's insights in the letters. But few have looked seriously at this proposed book, which as Bethge says carried him through the days of the failures of the conspiracy, with new arrests and executions going on around him. 'What he was writing then did not involve a struggle against Hitler. Hitler was no longer worthy to be dealt with theologically. It was the future task of the Church which entirely engaged Bonhoeffer's attention.'[11]

His book was to be addressed to the future, to those who had not been involved in the church struggle, even to those who were not yet born. In *Bonhoeffer: Exile and Martyr*, Eberhard Bethge has a chapter which attempts to fill out the 'Outline'.[12] It is necessary to look first of all at what the man closest to Bonhoeffer, the recipient of his letters and his confidence, says of this 'unwritten book'.

AUTHENTIC THEOLOGY

'Authentic Theology' is the title which Bethge gives to the chapter containing his treatment of Bonhoeffer's 'Outline'. He writes about the *Letters and Papers from Prison* and points out that Bonhoeffer developed a different approach in the later letters. The process of that change is explained by Bonhoeffer himself in the poem 'Stations on the Road to Freedom'.[13] He had experienced discipline and worldly responsibility. Now he begins to use phrases that have since become current in theological debate – 'non-religious interpretation', 'religionless Christianity', 'world come of age', 'arcane discipline', 'Jesus the man for others', 'the church for others'.[14] In popular debate such concepts are seen as changing theology into anthropology; but Bethge maintains that 'all of these are concerned in the fullest sense with theology'. In fact Bonhoeffer now raises the question of an 'authentic theology' more intensely than ever before. The 'Outline' is of a theological work, not an alternative to theology.

He does not start with 'Christology', however, as he would have done ten years before. The idea of establishing other points of departure (anathema to the Confessing Church, which under the guidance of Karl Barth saw the danger of admitting any other source of revelation) no longer worried him. Bonhoeffer was confident of the presence of Christ and was deeply concerned with the proclamation of the gospel. Therefore his interest focused on the proclaimer and the person addressed. Writing to Bethge, in reference to preaching, he said, 'One has to live for some time in a community to understand how Christ is "formed" in it (Gal. 4.19)'.[15] This 'Outline' insists that we begin 'Out there', with the freedom that comes from confidence in Christ, the freedom to see and dare to judge in the realm of secular history. 'Why should faith', he asks, 'prevent our eyes from being opened to see what there is, what there will be and what will pass away?'[16] The believer is not blinded by his faith; on the contrary, he sees more clearly what is happening in the secular world, because he believes in the Lord of all creation.

Inexorably, Bonhoeffer was driven to recognise that the church made a great mistake by opposing 'secularisation'. 'The attack by Christian apologetic on the adulthood of the world I consider to be in the first place pointless, in the second place ignoble, and in the third place unchristian.'[17] His phrase 'the adulthood of the world' came into use, as Bethge points out, after Bonhoeffer had read Wilhelm Dilthey in 1944 and derived from him the concept of 'maturity'. Earlier, he had written of the modern world as in the process of coming of age, but usually with regard to its becoming independent of the Church. The Renaissance had shown 'modern' man shaking off his tutelage to the church and struggling for autonomy, but in the summer of 1944 Bonhoeffer's reading of Dilthey led him to see 'the world coming of age' as human maturity.

WORLD COME OF AGE

The notion of a world 'come of age' is where Bonhoeffer intended to start his book. He sees it as the point of departure of modern man from the stagnated church. The pointless and ignoble attempt to push the world back into its adolescence, so that the church may retain its control over the daily life of humanity, results in scientific humanism or even communism being preferred as supporters of modern man against the obscurantism of the churches. This refusal to rejoice at the maturity of humanity is theologically unsound and unchristian! It confuses Christ with one particular stage in humanity's religious development. The contemporary world cannot be compared with the world of the Bible. Then, humanity worshipped, even if they worshipped idols. Now we do not even worship idols! In that fruitful summer of 1944 Bonhoeffer turned his attention to many aspects of theology, and everywhere he turned he was led back to the religionless state of the contemporary world. But he saw this as a stage in humanity's religious development, not as a regression. He watched in sorrow while the church contended against those who should have been its allies, and he particularly deplored the treatment of Darwin. 'God is being increasingly pushed out of a world that has come of age, out of the spheres of our knowledge and life . . .'[18]

It is because of this situation that Bonhoeffer's 'theological book' begins with a stocktaking[19] – and begins out there, where the church should be rejoicing at scientific progress instead of deploring secularisation. The first necessity, he says, will be to explore the nature of this maturity which affects philosophy, science, law and even religion. For Bonhoeffer, maturity is a human right, which if withheld is bound to do harm both to those from whom it is withheld and to those who withhold it. Thus, the ignoble role of trying to find areas of life where men and women cannot manage on their own, but need the church, leads to a diminution both of the church and humanity. For two hundred years the power of the Enlightenment deprived the church of its lordship over humanity. Bit by bit it surrendered its territory to reason. Science explained, where once the church proclaimed a miracle. It is therefore ignoble to grub around and find a place for God where science has so far not solved its problems. As this maturation process continued the church fought a rearguard

action, because this maturity of humanity was a threat to its
role as guardian and mediator. Bonhoeffer wants us to see
that this maturity is a good human right, good for the sake of
God and of Christ. Our obedience to the law of Christ, which
is the law of love, remains as part of our maturity; but this law
is not tutelage to keep humanity in bondage. Men and women
in their maturity are responsible and take responsibility for
their mistakes and rejoice at their successes.

Bonhoeffer caricatures the pastoral counsellors who sniff
around like investigative journalists to find out what is wrong
with a person who is happy! 'If he cannot be brought to see
and admit that his happiness is really an evil, his health
sickness, and his vigour despair, the theologian is at his wits'
end.'[20] Bonhoeffer's concept of maturity is a blow for freedom. The way in which the world lives and deals with itself,
the laws it discovers in science, the handling of political life,
the arts, ethics and even religion are free from tutelage to the
church.

This must not be confused with a belief in progress. Maturity is a stage in human development, not a guarantee that
all will be well. The early stage of human development was
concerned with battling against nature. 'Accidents' and
'blows of fate' – what insurance companies call 'acts of God' –
cannot be eliminated, but the danger can be reduced. Insurance, a Western phenomenon, lives on 'accidents' but seeks
to reduce their effects. Nature was formerly conquered by
spiritual means. We subdue it now by technical organisations
of every kind. Our immediate environment is no longer
nature, but organisation. What protects us against organisation? That question throws us back upon ourselves. We have
managed to deal with everything except ourselves. We can
insure against everything, but not against ourselves. In the
last resort it all depends upon us.

RELIGIONLESSNESS

Bonhoeffer moves on in his outline to look at the 'religionlessness of man come of age'.[21] In this context Bonhoeffer means

by 'religion' a complex of quite distinct ideas and views about God which he finds untenable in the light of modern scientific knowledge and also difficult to deduce directly from the scriptures. He observes that the working hypothesis of 'God' is no longer needed in the running of the world's affairs. He rejects the use of 'God' as a stop-gap while our knowledge catches up with our needs. Human society no longer needs religion to explain the world or to support humanity. Of course it still uses religion, but in a way that is unreal and not related to important activities. What runs the world today and explains it for the majority of people is not religion. In this sense, religion has had its day. That does not mean that the time of Christ has passed. Bonhoeffer is able to make these dangerous statements and still not lose his faith in God because it is built upon his absolute conviction that Christ lives. All his efforts are to discover who Christ is for modern man. It is only by recognising that modern Western society is no longer religious that he stands any chance of getting an answer to this persistent question 'Who is Jesus Christ for us today?' Neither has he abandoned the great Christian doctrines, although he finds they need a new interpretation.

Only three months earlier he sent a sermon to Bethge for the baptism of his first child, Dietrich Wilhelm Rüdiger Bethge, saying to the baby:

> Today you will be baptized a Christian. All those great ancient words of the Christian proclamation will be spoken over you . . . without your knowing anything about it. But we are once again being driven right back to the beginnings of our understanding. Reconciliation and redemption, regeneration and the Holy Spirit, love of our enemies, cross and resurrection, life in Christ and Christian discipleship – all these things are so difficult and so remote that we hardly venture any more to speak of them. In the traditional words and acts we suspect that there may be something quite new and revolutionary, though we cannot as yet grasp or express it.[22]

He goes on in that sermon to explain why. He points out that in the struggle of his day, the church has been fighting for its own preservation. Therefore the use of these traditional words has lost its force. He expresses his conviction that this self-preservation of the church has limited the role of the Christian, hindering true prayer and righteous action. He believes that it is only when sufficient Christians have by prayer and action rediscovered themselves that the church will be re-formed. A new form for the church will be born out of this prayer and action. He recognises that any premature attempt to reorganise the church would be fatal. But he is convinced that the time will come when the church in its new form will find a way to understand the great Christian verities in terms intelligible to its contemporaries in the world. Until that time comes, the Christian cause will be a silent one, a hidden affair, praying and doing right, waiting for God's time. And he hopes this child will see it.

THE PROTESTANT CHURCH

Bonhoeffer was a Lutheran, and his experiences of the years of National Socialism had been from within the Protestant Church. He knew the attractions of Rome, particularly in its liturgy, and he had learnt from the spirituality of Anglican religious communities. His ecumenical experience had led him to understand and appreciate churches of all traditions. But essentially he remained a Lutheran. When he turns from the world come of age, and the religionlessness of man who has come of age, to the church, he looks squarely at the Lutheran Church. He had seen the Protestant Church in Germany react to the upheavals of the Nazi regime by traditional pietism, by the reassertion of orthodoxy and by the Confessing Church, in whose struggle he had participated. He saw, looking back further in German history, that in all the upheavals of the world, the church had tried to secure a religious sphere for itself and prove itself indispensable to the world. But by this very act the church had become a watchdog of religion, an institution catering for marginal human problems – privileged, but shut away from the world's major problems. In his 'Outline' Bonhoeffer defines the decisive factor to be dealt with at this point as 'the church on the defensive. No taking risks for others.'[23]

Finally, to end the first part of his proposed book, he adds a fourth section: 'Public morals – as shown by sexual behaviour.'

'PUBLIC MORALS – AS SHOWN BY SEXUAL BEHAVIOUR'

This is a very difficult entry to interpret. We can be sure that Bonhoeffer did not intend to repeat the old clichés about declining standards, or to deplore sex before marriage or to denounce homosexuality. We have a corrective to that kind of thinking in his *Ethics*. His long section against the older ethical rules as inadequate to face the monstrous evil of his day is enough to guide us away from such trivia.[24] He does not hesitate to say that man is a sinner, but for Bonhoeffer man's sin lies not in these weaknesses which can be spied out, not in the personal failures which dominate so much of Protestant values, but in man's strength. Goethe and Napoleon were sinners, not because they were unfaithful husbands, but because of the way they used their strength. Bonhoeffer uses the phrase '*public* morals'. He hazards a guess at these sins of strength: 'in the genius, *hubris*; in the peasant, the breaking of the order of life . . . ; in the bourgeois, fear of free responsibility'.[25] Had he written that book, Bonhoeffer would, at this point, have confronted us with the judgement of God at our strongest point, not in our weaknesses.

THE MEANING OF THE CHRISTIAN FAITH

When Bonhoeffer disposed of 'religion', he never intended to do away with faith in God. Rather, he was clearing away the debris so that we might approach God. The second part of his 'Outline' deals with faith in God, the Christian faith in God.[26] This is nothing less than an attempt to build a new foundation for Christian faith.

First, God and the secular. Bonhoeffer is not original in wanting to set God free from the fetters of religion. He finds an unexpected ally in the great Bengali poet Rabindranath Tagore:

> Leave this chanting and singing and telling of beads!
> Whom dost thou worship in this lonely dark corner of a
>   temple with doors all shut?
> Open thine eyes and see thy God is not before thee!
> He is there where the tiller is tilling the soil and where the
>   roadmender is breaking stones.
> He is with them in sun and in shower, and his garment is
>   covered with dust.
> Put off thy holy mantle and even like him come down on
>   the dusty soil![27]

The question of God has to be answered in relation to the world. We must learn to speak of God in a worldly way. After all, the gospel says, 'God so loved *the world*'; who are we to despise it?

This will mean getting away from abstract arguments about God. It will mean following God's way and meeting him as we encounter Jesus in the world. There Christ is 'the man for others'. Christian faith is then defined as participating in this being of Jesus. This means getting away from a false transcendence, a 'religious' relationship to God, and into an existence for others, participating in the being of Jesus. The transcendental is not for Bonhoeffer the achievement of 'infinite and unattainable tasks', but relating to 'the neighbour who is within reach in any given situation': *transcendence in the midst*. On this basis he proposes to reinterpret the biblical concepts such as 'creation, fall, atonement, repentance, faith, the new life, the last things'. And those he follows with a suggestion that we look again at worship ('Cultus'). There the 'Outline' is less helpful, because he simply says: 'details to follow later'!

But he hurries on to a much larger section on telling the truth, or as Bethge puts it, 'stressing the honesty of mature faith'.[28] Honesty and authenticity grow 'where a mature Christian speaks himself, where he no longer entrenches himself behind tradition, creed or symbols'. Christian faith must be set free from every ideology.

What we have to face up to is the question 'What do we really believe?' That is the real question, not 'What *must* I believe?' The creeds have robbed us of our honesty. It is in this section that Bonhoeffer would have us deal with ecumenical relations. Interconfessional disputes are games, not to do with faith at all. Karl Barth comes in for criticism here, because he and the Confessing Church had said that we must entrench ourselves behind the 'faith of the church'. Bonhoeffer is convinced that in this we fall into a clericalist subterfuge – 'evade the honest question as to what we ourselves really believe'. Nothing can 'absolve us from the duty of being honest with ourselves'.

CONSEQUENCES FOR THE CHURCH

Bonhoeffer simply calls this part 'Conclusions'. The details show that it is to be entirely devoted to the form the church must take in the world. There are bold details in it from the start:

> The church is the church only when it exists for others. To make a start, it should give away all its property to those in need. The clergy must live solely on the free-will offerings of their congregations, or possibly engage in some secular calling. The church must share in the secular problems of ordinary human life . . .[29]

And so it goes on.

The theme in this part is the church and its transformation – so we are not to suppose that 'religionless Christianity' means a Christianity without a church. The first sentence in this part of the outline was adopted in 1968 as a slogan for the Fourth Assembly of the World Council of Churches at Uppsala: 'The Church is the Church only when it exists for others.' It was matched by the theme of that Assembly, taken from the book of Revelation: 'Behold I make all things new.' Bonhoeffer intended this final part to be about the renewal of the church, not its demise. We do not need to follow too closely the detailed suggestions he made for the life of the church in a world come of age and without religion, but we need to consider them. Our situation is different, but if we reject his details we must find our own.

Bonhoeffer's suggestions have been called naive, or, to use Bethge's word, 'unsophisticated',[30] but they are never trivial. The church must serve, not dominate. It must tell men of all kinds what it means to live in Christ, to exist for others. But far more important than what it 'tells' is its example. It is not abstract argument, but human example which gives the church credibility. It must fight against the vices of *hubris*, the worship of power, envy and humbug within the church itself. It must speak of course, but of 'moderation, purity, trust, loyalty, constancy, patience, discipline, humility, contentment, and modesty'.

When he goes further and suggests revising the creeds, Christian apologetics and training for the ministry, as well as the pattern of clerical life, Bonhoeffer becomes aware that the summary is running out and that he has no time to tidy it up. He adds to his 'Outline' the comment: 'All this is very crude and condensed, but there are certain things that I'm anxious to say simply and clearly – things that we so often like to shirk.'[31] He intended to go on, to discuss it all with Eberhard Bethge, and to write what he called 'the more constructive part', for the sake of the church of the future.

In the writing of my book, I am aware that Bonhoeffer has given me a great deal to work on and a splendid example in his own life. But at the end of the day, I have to write it myself for the church of my generation.

We are now that church of the future and this book is an attempt to do what he intended and was given neither peace nor strength to accomplish. Much has happened since his death and the thinking of the church has been influenced by his writings to a considerable extent. Yet he has more to say and it is the purpose of this book to take his insights into our generation and explore their relevance within the context of his 'Outline'.

Part 1

The Stocktaking of Christianity

INTRODUCTION

The dominant civilisation in the world is European. That civilisation has two major branches, both derived from Judaeo-Christian roots. They are Western capitalism and communism.

Such a bald statement would rightly appear arrogant to an Asian or an African. It may before long cease to be true. Islamic fundamentalism may conquer the world one day, but it has not yet; Japanese finance may control the world before long, but it is derived from Western capitalism. China may grow into a world-making civilisation with all the experience of its centuries of culture, but its first signs of growth are strongly influenced by the financial structures of Europe and America. At this point in human development European civilisation in both its forms has an overwhelming influence over the population of the earth.

Bonhoeffer was aware of this when he concentrated upon the Christianity into which he was born. What he could not be aware of was how European and American civilisation would develop after the war. He believed that European civilisation would survive, and it was because of this that he prayed for the defeat of his country. He had known Europe plundered by fascism and threatened by Bolshevism. He could not know that the Soviet Union would emerge as a superpower comparable with America, before which Western Europe itself would appear weak. We, however, *do* know that a new pattern has emerged in the power-structure of the world, and in the light of that knowledge we must take stock with Bonhoeffer's insights. He looked to a Europe after the war; we must look to a world approaching the year 2000. And like him our major concern is with Christianity. Can it survive in that world, and what will be the new form of its survival? He had no doubt that it would survive; but equally he had no doubt that it would have to be in a new form. The death of Christianity would be the attempt to retain its form without regard to the changing world around it. While waiting for God's time, the Christian cause *may* have to be 'a silent one, a hidden affair, praying and doing right', but the church must beware lest that chrysalis become a tomb.

The time of waiting appears to be over, and it is time for us to take stock and see what form the church will have in our new world. It is a polarised world, capable and in danger of destroying itself. The warning of God is heard in Hiroshima, in Chernobyl and in the meetings between superpowers. In a world which is just as much at war as it was when Bonhoeffer died, we must assess the role of European Christianity.

1

THE COMING OF AGE OF MANKIND

Today we look at ourselves, our world and God in ways that are radically different from the biblical views, whether of the Old or the New Testament. Biblical Christians are thus in danger of developing a split personality. In church we sing, pray and listen to sermons, all of which assume that God is in control of the universe, that he made a perfect world which man by his disobedience damaged, and that he forgives and offers to put it all right. We worship such a God and are deeply moved by a liturgy which praises him and accepts that we are totally dependent upon him for all our needs. We may even go so far as to say that if only we trusted him we should have no problems – 'Take it to the Lord in prayer'. Then we leave that 'shell of worship' and live quite differently in the outside world. There we know that we are responsible and that if we make a mess of our job we must take the consequences. In church we have said, 'He heals all your diseases', but when we are ill we go to the doctor. If we are mentally ill we go to a psychiatrist or a counsellor. In church we read, 'take no thought for the morrow', but if we acted like that we know that we should end up homeless and penniless, so we take out an insurance policy, calculate the mortgage we can afford, and pay our taxes with care that we do not pay too much. In all this God has no part. The world runs itself without God.

This schizophrenic situation is the result of a long process.

For centuries men and women believed in God, and he had a part in every aspect of their lives. Few things were done without prayer. The vagaries of nature depended upon his benevolence. The soil may be ploughed well, the best seed planted, the birds driven away from the new growth, but in the end, 'God giveth the increase'. That was the Bible view, and that was the view of the Middle Ages. All depended upon God, and he was mediated through the church, whose priests were the custodians of his treasury. That is no longer our view, even if we still profess it in the church.

THE PROGRESS OF MATURITY

Somewhere around the thirteenth century, the exact date does not matter, there was a stirring in European civilisation which we usually call the Renaissance. It flowered in painting, sculpture, literature and a spirit of confidence. The human race seemed to discover its potential. The church had mediated the Bible, now people demanded that they see what the Bible says and judge for themselves. Wycliffe and his Lollard priests made the Bible available in a language that all could understand. Even the illiterate could hear and understand. There was an upsurge of the human person demanding autonomy. Man wanted to be master of his own life, although he was not always as willing to grant the same autonomy to his wife or his daughter! (There were outstanding women of the Renaissance, but largely it was a man's world.)

The confidence had come from many sources, but important among them was a rediscovery of the Bible. Until then the church had interpreted it to retain control over the people. Christ had given the power of the keys to Peter, and through him to the church. The church could forgive or refuse to forgive. The church could hold or withold the body of Christ, by which alone men were redeemed from hell. The church had unlimited power, even beyond the grave. But the Bible spoke of liberty, freedom, the breaking of chains: 'The Sabbath was made for man, not man for the Sabbath.' And even in the Old Testament the dignity of man was preached: '. . . a little less than God'. Man was the crown of God's creation, his deputy on earth. The men of the Renaissance explored the human spirit and found it good – poetry, music, dance, health, science and knowledge of all kinds. These were not mysteries to be ministered to good boys if they kept the law. They were to be found out by courageous effort and the exercise of the mind. Life became experimental. You have only to read the life of someone like Leonardo da Vinci or Michelangelo to feel the pulse of excitement as new worlds opened up. And there were literally new worlds, as explorers spanned the world with courage towards what they had previously believed was an abyss. The old science of the church was proved wrong, and men sailed round the world.

Science was born anew and there was no loss of faith, simply a loss of the church's credibility. When the storm of the Renaissance had subsided, the church counted its losses and came to a compromise. There were areas of life where it could concede human independence; but it would retain the great mysteries and whole areas of uncharted experience which science could not touch. Every new advance of knowledge was then resisted by the church until it could be fitted within its own dogmatic framework of truth.

It was an adolescent period for the human race – at least in Europe. Science proceeded to win its victories. But plagues still beset Europe – and famine, when harvests failed. Men and women were dependent upon what we call nature, but that meant for them the apparently arbitrary decisions of God. Nature could be subdued only by supernatural means. Man may be lord of creation, disposer of the lower creatures, but God was still in control, and the church was needed for disasters and for death. Science's writ did not run beyond the grave. And the mind too had frontiers beyond which science could not pass.

It was a comfortable compromise. Man felt his greatness – although he was a miserable sinner in church, where he obtained absolution at a price. With this supernatural guarantee behind him, he could do almost anything. He was the crown of creation, with all creatures subject to his command; his world lay at the centre of the universe, whose stars rotated round him like some glorious nightly pageant. The church kept his pride within bounds and preserved him from the punishments of *hubris* (pride) which the Greeks had feared.

This spirit continued for some time as the church exercised authority over any attempts to disturb it.

THE EDIFICE TOPPLES

Three hammer-blows shattered the complacency of such a world-view.

Copernicus and *Galileo* showed conclusively that the earth was not at the centre of the universe. It circulated round the sun and was part of that pageant – not round man and his world but round the sun. Later, even that sun was shown to be quite ordinary. The church did its best to suppress the truth; but it was out. Man's unique position in the universe was no longer tenable geographically.

After the Reformation had weakened the church's control of human exploration, both Protestant and Catholic churches became fearful of what man might uncover. Too much science was looked upon with suspicion, and the experimenters were often condemned by both sides for impious exploration into God's secrets!

Charles Darwin delivered the next hammer-blow in the middle of the nineteenth century, when Protestant churches, as arrogant as Rome, held man in thrall. The biblical teaching which had set men free was now used to limit their freedom. What the Bible taught must be accepted regardless of what the human mind had discovered. Darwin gave to the human species a very high place in the evolutionary scheme. The human species was the result of many trials and errors. Humanity had evolved as *the* success. But Darwin linked the human grandeur to the animal ancestry and offended against the accepted biblical teaching. A special creation was defended – if not unique in his creation, how can evolution explain the entry of the soul into man? If man was only the best of the animals, he might acquire honour, but his uniqueness was gone. It also followed from what Darwin uncovered that evolution had not yet finished. This contradicted the six-day creation and God declaring it very good. A perfect world damaged by man's disobedience and the fall did not fit into the theory of evolution. And worse, if God has not finished, he may yet do better than the human species. This thought was taken up later by Teilhard de Chardin, but in the nineteenth century few churchmen and even fewer bishops were prepared to entertain this radical shock to the human system.

Sigmund Freud accepted Darwin's conclusions as self-evident and then proceeded to deliver a third hammer-blow. He explored the mind and crossed sacred frontiers. He left the drawing-room of the human house and explored the cellar. There he discovered that the human heart was desperately wicked, as the Bible said, but in the unconscious there were very many disagreeable things that could not be dealt with in the confessional or at the penitence stool. The neurosis of humanity was seen as beyond reasonable control. Criminals could not be cured by punishment nor saints cleared of shameful thoughts. Even children were shown steeped in sexual degradation. The conflict with Freud has a particular interest for us because, although he rejected Christianity, he saw the roots of religion in all people. His treatment of religion is germane to our book.

FREUD'S CRITIQUE OF RELIGION

Freud sees art, philosophy and religion as the three powers which might dispute the basic superiority of science. But only religion is to be taken seriously as an enemy. For him, 'religion is an immense power which has the strongest emotions of human beings at its service'. He believes it is an illusion, but recognises that it took the place of science before that had developed. It constructed a world-view (*Weltanschauung*), consistent and self-contained. Although this latter had been severely shaken by science, Freud does not write it off. Religion supplies the needs of humanity by giving information about the origin and coming into being of the universe; it offers protection and ultimate happiness in the ups and downs of life, and it directs thoughts and actions by precepts which are laid down with its whole authority. This threefold function, which Freud examines closely, brings religion into conflict with science in its first function (satisfying the thirst for knowledge); outstrips science in its second (protection and promise of ultimate happiness); and bears no relation to science in its third (directing thoughts and actions by precepts). He thus sees that religion is the strongest contender, but it is an illusion. Therefore Freud chooses truth, which he believes can be found only in objective, scientific observation.

After very careful analysis Freud establishes to his own satisfaction that religion belongs to the childhood of humanity and must be dispersed with maturity. Religious views are survivals into adulthood of the helplessness of children. Parent-dependence becomes dependence upon God. Here is Freud's summary in his last lecture of the *New Introductory Lectures on Psychoanalysis*:

> While the different religions wrangle with one another as to which of them is in possession of the truth, our view is that the question of the truth of religious beliefs may be left altogether on one side. Religion is an attempt to master the sensory world in which we are situated by means of the wishful world which we have developed within us as a result of biological and psychological necessities. But religion cannot achieve this. Its doctrines bear the imprint of the time in which they arose, the ignorant times of the childhood of humanity. Its consolations deserve no trust. Experience teaches us that the world is no nursery. The ethical demands on which religion seeks to lay stress need, rather, to be given another basis; for they are indispensable to human society and it is dangerous to link obedience to them with religious faith. If we attempt to assign the place of religion in the evolution of mankind, it appears not as a permanent acquisition but as a counterpart to the neurosis which individual civilized men have to go through in their passage from childhood to maturity.[1]

It is not necessary to accept totally that criticism of religion in order to recognise its importance. Sigmund Freud in the 1930s was in fact following a path parallel to that which Dietrich Bonhoeffer would follow some ten years later. Both have to deal with the maturity of humanity, the outgrowing of religion and the residual elements of childhood in the mature person.

The reaction of the church to Freud was almost totally hostile. Not quite totally, because one Protestant pastor saw his value for pastoral work, almost from the beginning. Oscar Pfister of Zürich surprised Freud by his acceptance of much that the latter said. He compelled Freud to see that his discoveries could be of value to the church in its work. Bonhoeffer's father, who was in the same field of studies, refused to publish Freud's article and closed his mind to Freud's ideas.

Copernicus was accepted; Darwin was being reluctantly admitted as an honest scientist, however, colour-blind to biblical truths; Freud was too much. The church fell back upon its authority, its Bible and its doctrines. While all three disturbers of the peace gained ground and proved themselves in the general progress of human knowledge, the church remained – privileged, but isolated from the scientific understanding of humanity.

THE MATURING OF SCIENCE

Bonhoeffer was already aware that science was changing and had lost a little of its confidence about 'objective reality'. In his letter of 16 July 1944, when he attempted to trace the growth of the world's autonomy historically, he adds in brackets:

> It seems that in the natural sciences the process begins with Nicholas of Cusa and Giordano Bruno and the 'heretical' doctrine of the infinity of the universe. The classical *cosmos* was finite, like the created world of the Middle Ages. An infinite universe, however it may be conceived, is self-subsisting, *etsi deus non daretur* [as though God were not there]. It is true that modern physics is not as sure as it was about the infinity of the universe, but it has not gone back to the earlier conceptions of its finitude.[2]

Bonhoeffer grew up in a household where conversation was more often about the arts and sciences than about theology. He was well informed about the general attitudes and achievements of the science in his day. Since his time progress has been even faster and the achievements greater. One need only mention the placing of men on the moon, the rapid advances in computer science, transistors and satellite broadcasting. But at the same time theoretical physics has become less certain of the truth of its own observations. Few physicists would claim 'objective reality' for the results of their observations. The scientific world has also matured these fifty years since the outbreak of the Second World War.

In two fields the old order has been challenged and defended, while the application of science in ever-growing technology has progressed without interruption. The fields are those of microbiology and physics. Both in the examination of the smallest particles and in the exploration of the universe, physics has asked questions about the relation of its conclusions to reality. Technology has used the results, and they work, thereby giving to science great credibility. But physicists have continually asked whether their description of matter or the universe bears any relation to reality. Have they working models or a perception of truth?

In order to confine this treatment to modest proportions, let me select four scientists who have contributed to the maturing of science since Bonhoeffer wrote his letters from prison.

Jacques Monod, a microbiologist, in his book *Chance and Necessity* has convincingly argued for an emergence and evolution of the human species which is based upon a mindless repetition of existing forms, interrupted by chance changes which are in turn repeated. The human species is an accident faithfully repeated, and there is no outside assistance for this development. Those who talk of a supernatural direction, or of the universe having a purpose, are disregarding the plain truths of science.

His position is clearly put in strong words: 'The universe was not pregnant with life nor the biosphere with man. Our number came up in the Monte Carlo game. Is it surprising that, like the person who has just made a million at the casino, we should feel strange and a little unreal?[3] On the basis of his thesis, Monod can say only that we have a choice and that no outside power can help us, 'we are gypsies on the rim of the universe'. The picture is bleak but not hopeless. Its strength lies in its logical coherence alone. For him, there is only one conclusion to which science (*i.e.*, the search for authenticity) necessarily leads:

> The ancient covenant is in pieces; man at last knows that he is alone in the unfeeling immensity of the universe, out of which he emerged only by chance. neither his destiny nor his duty have been written down. The kingdom above or the darkness below: it is for him to choose.[4]

That is not a picture that Bonhoeffer could have accepted, but he was prepared to face it.

Teilhard de Chardin, whose writings were not published until after Bonhoeffer's execution, was one of the targets for Jacques Monod. He was a palaeontologist and a Jesuit. His search into the past left him unsatisfied, because he was never explaining anything. He was giving a sense of order to a chaotic past. This led him to look at the apparent forward direction of evolution – not from what it had emerged, but to what it was progressing. When the picture was turned upside down in this way, he saw purpose in the progress of all creation: from inanimate to living, from simple forms of life to complexity, from life to mind, from the blind reaction to phenomena to complexity and consciousness, from diversity to unity. He saw all creation, not in some mystic's dream, but in the facts of his science, moving towards a fulfilment.[5] Many said he was deluding himself – Jacques Monod and Peter Medawar both saw him as a dreamer rather than a scientist. But Julian Huxley, the foremost biologist of his day, saw what for years he had searched, a mechanism which explained evolution. At least Teilhard had to be taken into account as part of the scientific scene. And there are many physicists and microbiologists who take him seriously today.

Paul Davies, Professor of Theoretical Physics in Newcastle, whose researches have been mainly in the investigation of black holes, the origin of the universe and other aspects of fundamental physics, has argued for some emerging pattern in the universe. He calls his book *The Cosmic Blueprint*, but with an implied question mark. All he will say definitely is that there appears to be something going on behind the universe which resembles some kind of purpose. It is best to quote his conclusions, rather than pick up crumbs of hope from the occasional ideas he throws out. The whole book should be read, but here are his concluding words in the paragraphs headed, 'What does it all mean?':

> I believe that science is in principle able to explain the existence of complexity and organization at all levels, including human consciousness, though only by embracing the 'higher level' laws. Such a belief might be regarded as denying a god or purpose in this wonderful creative universe we inhabit. I do not see it that way. The very fact that the universe *is* creative, and that the laws have permitted complex structures to emerge and develop to the point of consciousness – in other words, that the universe has organized its own self-awareness – is for me powerful evidence that there is 'something going on' behind it all. The impression of design is overwhelming. Science may explain all processes whereby the universe evolves its own destiny, but that still leaves room for there to be a meaning behind existence.[6]

Much of this had already been developed earlier by Stanley Jaki[7] and others. Such an attitude would have strengthened rather than weakened Bonhoeffer's views of the 'coming of age' of man.

Sergei Tarassenko, a nuclear physicist of Russian origin, who worked for EURATOM on international thermonuclear fusion, goes further than Paul Davies. He maintains that science has 'unsurmountable limits', that what we perceive by scientific investigation is a reflection of our mind not a description of absolute reality: 'It is as if there were a barrier, which is admittedly moving forward with progress but which confines man within the "known".' That barrier he further defines as 'that totality of reflections on his perception of the universe which already makes him aware of the fundamental difference between the "known" and reality.'[8]

Tarassenko believes that only faith can cross the abyss from that projection of man which he has called the 'known' to reality. He has of course worked this out in great detail, not as some subjective view, but from his belief that he had been 'found by God'. His mission is now to oppose the tyranny of science, expose 'the Lie' that it is objective truth, 'to lift the corner of the impressive veil of technological progress to reveal the extent of the disaster'. This is not anti-science, nor a reactionary fear of knowledge, for he believes that the lie he is exposing 'has perverted the extraordinary capacity for Science which God has put into man for it to help him manage his planet'. He continues, 'This ability has been perverted because man has set up Science, a projection of himself, as a god.'

BONHOEFFER'S BEGINNINGS

It is necessary to go back to Bonhoeffer's important letter to Bethge of 8 June 1944.[9] Glancing back at the Renaissance, he saw how its surge towards the autonomy of man, the discovery of the laws by which the world deals with itself in science, politics, art, ethics and religion, means that for most people the 'working hypothesis' called 'God' is no longer necessary. In science, ethics and art, the battle is already lost. God has no place. But more serious developments that we have looked at in Darwin and Freud mean that this is also convincingly true of religious questions. Everything gets on quite well without God. God is being pushed more and more out of life, losing more and more ground. When this autonomy is resisted, it has the effect of turning progressive movements anti-Christian.

> The world that has become conscious of itself and the laws that govern its own existence . . . has grown self-confident in . . . an uncanny way. False developments and failures do not make the world doubt the necessity of the course it is taking, or of its development; they are accepted with fortitude and detachment as part of the bargain, and even an event like the present war is no exception.[10]

In its resistance to this growing maturity, the church has confused Christ with one particular stage in man's religious consciousness. Bonhoeffer pursues his question: Where is Christ in a world coming of age? And what is the significance of Christ in the maturing process? Liberal theology failed because it conceded to the world the right to determine how Jesus Christ is to be explained and define Christ's place in the world. 'The Jesus of history', or the many attempts to place Jesus of Nazareth in the historical process, failed. Liberal theology accepted the challenge, but lost and then conceded the peace terms dictated by the world. The church in Germany tried to make a fresh start, based upon the Bible and the Reformation. Bonhoeffer looks at certain theologians who in his lifetime had faced the crisis by urging the church to seek an authority not subject to the dictates of the world. Karl Heim drew upon the resources of pietism and tried to show modern man that he was faced with a choice – 'Jesus or despair'. It was an emotional appeal. Paul Althaus was prepared to follow the liberal line and let the world go along its own path, provided that it allowed a place for the Lutheran ministry and Lutheran worship. Paul Tillich attempted to interpret evolution, against its will, in a religious sense: God is in the process. He tried to give shape and purpose to the stream of evolution. It was a courageous act. Bonhoeffer comments: 'That was very brave of him, but the world unseated him and went on by itself; he, too, sought to understand the world better than it understood itself . . .'[11] Tillich's failure is explained by Bonhoeffer as the correct attempt, but the wrong means – the world *has* to be understood better than it understands itself, but *not* in a religious sense. All these attempts would later be seen as part of the complex known as liberal theology.

KARL BARTH AND THE CONFESSING CHURCH

So far, Bonhoeffer has been able to look at movements of which he was not really a part. Now he turns to his own involvement. He was an enthusiastic Barthian, although never quite uncritical.

Karl Barth accused liberal theology of trying to make a space for religion in the world. He attacked religion in the name of the God of Jesus Christ. He launched his attack in the second edition (1921) of his commentary *The Epistle to the Romans*.[12] God was no *deus ex machina*, a god who comes from the wings like a theatrical trick to rescue careless people from the consequences of their carelessness. This is not the God of our Lord Jesus Christ. But Barth did not sustain this strong line in his *Church Dogmatics*, and his critics said that he failed eventually in his treatment of ethics. Bonhoeffer is not fully convinced of this judgement, although he does not adequately defend Barth's ethics, and his own writing certainly takes a very different line. His accusation against Barth's theology is, however, of another kind. Barth was quite unable to give any help in the non-religious interpretation of theological concepts. He was not prepared to leave the church without legitimate independent ground in the world. Bonhoeffer's assessment was that Barth had gone so far in his rejection of religious language, but was not prepared to go the whole length of religionless Christianity. Instead he fell back on 'revelation'. He too was a positivist; his was a 'positivism of revelation'.[13]

Karl Barth was successful in convincing the Confessing Church that they should reject the heresy that there could be any other revelation. The German Christians had maintained that God had revealed his will for Germany through Adolf Hitler. Thanks to Barth the Confessing Church opposed this, but they forgot the lively aspect of his theology and fell back into 'conservative restoration'. This was Bonhoeffer's phrase for the concentration of the Confessing Church upon the great concepts of Christian theology. Quite good in itself, but not if it leaves the church exhausted.

Rudolf Bultmann saw Barth's limitations, but Bonhoeffer also found him wanting. At heart Bultmann was an old-fashioned liberal, and his demythologising programme was a form of liberal reductionism. He was not the man to lead the Confessing Church out of its isolation. Bonhoeffer did not see Bultmann as too radical, but not radical enough. It is not enough to remove the mythological elements and reduce the gospel to its 'essence'. Bonhoeffer expressed his view briefly: 'the full content, including the "mythological" concepts, must be kept – the New Testament is not a mythological clothing of a universal truth; this mythology (resurrection etc.) is the thing itself'.[14] But he admits that these concepts have to be interpreted. Then comes his own emphasis. They must be interpreted in such a way as 'not to make religion a precondition of faith'.[15] Paul had a similar task to do for a Jewish church. He had to preach a gospel which did not make circumcision a condition of faith. What we have to do, who have recognised that the world has come of age, is so to interpret the myths of redemption that they are realised this side of the grave. In order to do this we need to hold the Old Testament and the New Testament together.

The Old Testament, as Bonhoeffer discusses in the letter of 27 June 1944,[16] has redemption at the centre of its message, but not a mythological redemption to be realised after death. Old Testament redemption, whether from Egypt or Babylon, is historical. Israel is delivered out of Egypt so that it may live before God as God's people on earth. And this is what distinguishes the Christian hope of resurrection from a mythological hope. It sends a person back to earth, to life in the world, living in a new way. The Christian, unlike the devotee of the redemption myths, has no escape from his earthly tasks and difficulties into an eternal world. Like Christ he must drink the earthly cup to the dregs – even to the extent of being forsaken by God. Bonhoeffer's strong contrast between Christian redemption by union with Christ in his life, crucifixion and resurrection, and the redemption myths, is the basis of his understanding of the Christian life lived in a world come of age. The contrast is summed up in the sentence, 'Redemption myths arise from human boundary-experiences, but Christ takes hold of a man at the centre of his life.'[17] What really concerned Bonhoeffer as he saw the church refusing to accept the implications of a world come of age was that he wanted to claim the world for Christ; not some imaginary world as it ought to be, but the world as it is – the world come of age. Now this claim cannot be made if the Christian withdraws from the world into a religious enclave.

Daniel Jenkins, in his book *Beyond Religion*, which assesses the truth and error in 'Religionless Christianity', shows

the dangers of withdrawal into religious activities unless we
know what we are doing. If we think that the world (in the
pejorative sense) cannot reach us when engaged in these
activities, we are mistaken. A withdrawal for such protection
is a capitulation to the world. It is to accept the fact that the
world is too strong to be overcome. Jenkins goes on:

> It is not an accident that the life of so many of the self-consciously
> pious enclaves of people who imagine that they have successfully
> contracted out of most of the evils of modern society in this world
> should be so notably narrow, repressive and stuffy. There are
> many such societies bearing a Christian name, both Protestant
> and Catholic, and the fact that the life they produce is so
> unsatisfactory, not least in the very self-satisfaction it produces
> among those who live it, is a challenge to Christian understanding
> and an obstacle to Christian belief.[18]

These withdrawn societies represent an unhealthy form of
worldliness, masking itself as unworldliness. There is a form
of withdrawal which is evidently needed, and the need is
recognised in modern society for sabbaticals and retreats.
These are needed by businessmen and women, politicians,
professionals, including clergy, and all who are involved in
the stress of modern living. They are not escapes, but times to
gather strength for more effective engagement in the world.

CONVERSION TO THE WORLD

H. H. Kraemer quotes a saying of the elder Blumhardt,
'Every Christian needs two conversions, first to Christ and
then to the world'.[19] When this is put side by side with an
article by Dr H. H. Walz in *The Ecumenical Review* (April
1958),[20] it is a powerful comment on the proper understanding of the relation of 'church' to 'world'. Walz writes that the
'autonomy' announced by the world is a misunderstanding of
itself; but 'heteronomy' (*i.e.* the control of the world from
outside) is the church's misunderstanding of the world. This
has been illustrated in post-war Europe in the development of
some form of 'welfare state' in many countries, notably in
northern Europe, including Britain. The acceptance of

responsibility by the state for the care of its people to such an extent as Lord Beveridge proposed in his report, and Attlee's Labour Government began to put into effect, inevitably 'secularised' many church activities. The growth of state schools which led to the weakening of private and church schools had much the same effect.

Similarly, secular bodies sometimes took over traditionally church organisations, as when a communist government was established in the DDR (East Germany). When that happens many churchmen regard it as a victory for Godless secularism. It can be that an atheist control denies the Lordship of God, but it can also be that a secular administration can express true Christian maturity in freedom. Loss of control by the church does not mean that God has been robbed of his Lordship. As the privileges of the church in society weaken, and as its control of organisations that form that society is taken out of its hands, there is an opportunity for growth and maturity. Christians in their maturity learn to identify. They recognise that they are part of the world which Christ came to save and that their role is to participate in his saving act. That means being with other human beings and working with them, whether they are Christians or not. Few who know the centuries of oppression that the poor in Latin America have suffered under Spanish (or Portuguese) Catholicism, and later under American Protestantism, will fail to be ashamed of the church-controlled enterprises.

When in recent years the poor have raised their heads, it has been Christians, working together with communists, who have raised the consciousness to the level of revolt. There can be little doubt that he whom John MacKay called 'the other Spanish Christ'[21] has been at work in the liberating of Latin America. And in this liberation Christians have identified themselves with Christ in his saving work, and done this side by side with those who do not believe in God. A Pope's disapproval has not prevented Catholics from continuing, nor has the withdrawal of funds by American missionary societies halted the work of American Protestants. Liberation theology has become the maturity of Christian theology in Latin America.

THE PRIVATISATION OF RELIGION

Bonhoeffer did not cease to believe that a believer meets Christ in the word, in the sacrament and in the *koinonia* of the church; but he also believed that he met Christ no less in those places 'where he has to take a decision which significantly determines his own and his neighbour's conduct, whether in work or in the public life or in private personal relationships'.[22]

Over the past few years there has been a debate in Britain over the 'privatisation' of religion. It was stirred up by a series of Reith lectures by Edward Norman.[23] The Anglicans in particular took sides. There were those who saw danger in spreading the activities of the church so thinly, commenting upon every issue of the day, taking stands, demonstrating, telling governments what they should do, demanding justice for the poor, *etc.* Their attitude was caricatured by Helder Câmara in his oft-repeated words: 'When I give food to the hungry, they say I am a saint; but when I ask why the hungry have no food, they say I am a trouble maker.'[24] Those who like Edward Norman advocate the privatisation of religion ask that churches do what they alone can do – worship, administer the sacraments, cultivate Christian fellowship, defend the faith and see that the nation is aware of the sovereignty of God in Christ, offering salvation and comforting the weak. Others who are more activist have insisted that the church may say clearly when the state is wrong, demand that it change its ways and in every way become a voice for the voiceless, the champion of the poor. These are 'social Christians' and they imperil the continuance of the church by estranging the support of the state. There is little doubt that maturity as Bonhoeffer understood it would mean accepting the loss of support for the sake of identification with the poor in the world.

2

SPIRITUAL RESOURCES

If humanity has reached a level of maturity comparable with a young person leaving home and no longer depending upon the support of parents, where does it find the spiritual resources to cope with itself? Nature is conquered. European civilisation no longer depends upon the vagaries of nature, but can produce more than enough to feed itself and the world. Mountains of food and lakes of wine and milk give evidence of the success of human technology and organisation. If there are still millions of people underfed and starving in Africa and Asia, it is because of the lack of will on the part of the rest of the world rather than inability. Nature has been conquered, not by prayer, but by what Bonhoeffer called 'technical organization'. Our environment is no longer the uncertain weather and threatened crops, but a humanly controlled organisation, computerised in a way that Bonhoeffer could hardly envisage. We are protected from nature's menace. But Bonhoeffer's question still remains: 'What protects us from the menace of organisation if the spiritual force is lacking?'[1]

THE CONTROLLING POWER OF THE ORGANISATION

In a highly technical and computerised society such as America or the democracies of Western Europe there is a growing sense of not being in control of one's life. Even at the simple level of computerised accounts it is much more difficult to argue with a computer than with an accountant. Decisions appear to be made by organisations rather than people. Of course the computer has no more information than a human feeds into it; but it can coordinate that material and draw conclusions from it far more quickly than a human mind can. A dimension of freedom has been lost. This is well illustrated by Stafford Beer in his books about business management. *The Brain of the Firm*,[2] the title of one of his books, does not apply to a person, but to a system. As interest rates rise and fall, as market forces determine whether an investment gains or loses value, there appears to be a system operating which bears no relationship to the world of personal decisions or achievements. Even those involved in the economic systems of the world, who are able to assess the way they are likely to move, are aware that they are not doing the moving, but merely detecting and predicting it.

Bonhoeffer knew the world of dictators who controlled the lives of people by their edicts; but they were people, however unpleasant and evil. There are no longer people to praise or blame, only to congratulate on success. Such a society has made the standard of living much higher for most people; it has removed a great deal of drudgery from work. But it has left casualties. The way in which we respond to these casualties is the evidence of a vestige of human responsibility in a world where it is more and more difficult to respond. The human mind was still an important instrument for assessing evidence and making decisions for future action well after the invention of the mechanical computer by Charles Babbage in 1820. But since 1946 the electrification of the computer has increased its speed of action a million times, and it will get faster. This leaves the human mind far behind. Having fed the computer, the person must take orders from it, because there is no alternative method of assessing the material. We have not yet abandoned human control. So far the upper echelons of managements (including government) are serviced by information about 'what has happened in the past – in the hope that this knowledge will somehow illuminate the darkness of an unknown future. Most attempts to look ahead then are concerned with the extrapolation of historic trends.'[3]

Stafford Beer, from whom that quote is taken, disapproves. He shows convincingly that management now has the tools for 'inventing the future, rather than fearfully predicting what it may hold'.

The problem is that management becomes the science of the elite who do not have to justify their decisions to the people. The system is in control. There is no point in deploring this development, any more than it was to deplore evolution. It is necessary to integrate it within the Christian view of the kingdom of God. What Teilhard de Chardin did with the exciting evidence of evolution must now be done with advances in our understanding of information flow. There is no reason why it should be allowed to pass out of democratic control. After all, the most complex information system has grown out of the TV set, the telephone and the typewriter, all three of which we have accepted as an enrichment of personal life. Not everyone can be expected to be trained in the higher complexities of business management, but enough can be understood to apply checks and balances that will enable the responsible individual to be able to judge harmful or healthy trends, good or evil, just or unjust. Thus when a government invents the future its casualties are our warning signs. If a booming economy is at the price of high unemployment, or if growth is achieved by impoverishing one part of the community, then the church does not argue on the basis of cybernetics but moral effects. This requires the working out of a system of ethics which is adaptable to the situation created by those who 'invent the future'.

It is important that the church should learn to fight on its own ground. Any attempt to put the economy back into an ancient form which it can understand and to which it can then apply established systems of ethics is fatal. The church should be able to accept and indeed welcome advances into the future which enable humankind to be responsible for its own future. But it should be careful to watch the effect upon the casualties. This is not to concentrate upon the failures, nor to condemn success. It is, however, to ask about the price of success in terms of human suffering and injustice. As it was right for Bonhoeffer, in the days of Jewish persecution, to say that those who did not shout for the Jews had no right to sing the Gregorian chants,[4] so it is right today to insist that those who are successful at the cost of their neighbour's poverty have no right to the support of the church in their enterprises. It is as sweet as singing the Gregorian chants for a business-man to uphold 'Victorian values' such as the proper use of Sunday, the drive for clean TV free of sex and violence, the protection of the unborn child or the denouncing of homo-sexuality as sin. But he has no right to do that unless he is caring for the casualties of the system which has made him successful. The building of a property-owning democracy, with the joy of home ownership, must be accompanied by dealing justly with the homeless and the young people unable to climb the ladder of success or the old people who left it too late. A compassionate society is not one that despises success, but one that cares for those who by its own terms are regarded as failures. True religion has three parts still, even though they were first demonstrated and expressed nearly three thousand years ago: 'What does the Lord require of you but to do justice, and to love kindness, and to walk humbly with your God?' (Micah 6:8). Justice, compassion, humility before God.

In the rather more restricted community of the early Chris-tian church this was spelt out in terms fitting the conditions of first-century Christianity: 'Religion that is pure and undefiled before God and the Father is this: to visit orphans and widows in their affliction, and to keep oneself unstained from the world' (James 1:27).

In a society where economic forces, flow of information, organisation of relationships are all taken out of the hands of individuals and are determined by the system, or 'organis-ation', the church has to learn how to address the people who are both its victims and its operators. In particular the church needs to be able to show what 'religion' means in this context. The danger is that it will be divorced from the context and become a private activity alone. The quotations from Micah and James give us some clue as to how we should proceed.

Compassion is a private activity and easily understood without arguments, whether it be expressed as 'to love kindness' or 'to visit orphans and widows in their affliction'. That will mean 'going beyond the call of duty' to assist the sufferers, and not distinguishing between the deserving and undeserving poor. Those in need make demands upon us regardless of their worth. The Good Samaritan did not pause to ask whether it was the man's own fault that he travelled alone on a dangerous road! There are many examples today of generous giving of time and money for those in need – the starving in Africa, the miners on strike, the homeless at Christmas, Nelson Mandela in prison – and such a wide variety that it would seem that we are a compassionate society when we see the need and are able to help.

The second element is expressed differently in the two periods of history. For Micah it is 'to do justice'; for James, 'to keep oneself unstained from the world'. The stain of the world is injustice. The system which is controlling us needs to be examined, and we who profit from it must examine ourselves to see whether it has stained us. Are we going with soiled hands to visit the widows and orphans? Is our generosity an easy way to avoid looking too closely at 'hands covered in blood'? 'Unstained' does not mean that we have done nothing, for silence too can be guilty. It means that we have not allowed the system to quieten our consciences by separating us from the decisions which are made.

The third element, which Micah defines as 'walking humbly with your God' and James builds into his statement as 'before God and the Father', is the recognition that we are not independent of God. Bonhoeffer made much of our coming of age, of our taking responsibility and not expecting God to come in from the wings to rescue us from our own foolish decisions; but he did not cut us off from God the Father. He saw that we had used religious statements without fully understanding their meaning, so that 'we hardly venture any more to speak of them'.[5] He saw the fault of his generation and his church, in that it had expended all its energies in protecting itself; but in that same address for the baptism of Dietrich Wilhelm Rüdiger Bethge he wrote significantly: 'In the traditional words and acts we suspect that there may be something quite new and revolutionary, though we cannot as yet grasp or express it.'[6] He advocated 'prayer and righteous action' while we wait for enlightenment. He did not advocate premature reform of the organisation of the church, because that would delay its conversion and purification. His vision of the future was clear at this point – and surely it is time for that vision to be realised:

> It is not for us to prophesy the day (though the day will come) when men will once more be called so to utter the word of God that the world will be changed and renewed by it. It will be a new language, perhaps quite non-religious, but liberating and redeeming . . .[7]

These words can only be spoken in freedom if we are unstained by the world, as Jesus was. This is not a matter of personal purity alone, it is a freedom which comes from not letting the 'organisation' control us. There is a hint in that baptismal address which shows something of the new freedom:

> We have spent too much time in thinking, supposing that if we weigh in advance the possibilities of any action, it will happen automatically. We have learnt, rather too late, that action comes not from thought, but from a readiness for responsibility. For you thought and action will enter on a new relationship; your thinking will be confined to your responsibilities in action. With us thought was often the luxury of the onlooker; with you it will be entirely subordinated to action.[8]

The importance of that prophetic paragraph grows immensely as we see the crucial decisions about the nature of our society removed further and further away from individual responsible action. To paraphrase Karl Marx: 'The experts have explained the system; it may now be time to change it by Christian responsible action.' And thus we are to be 'unstained by the world', remembering the humility before God with which we undertake such action.

THE RESPONSIBLE SELF

The writer who has most clearly accepted the challenge of Bonhoeffer's call for 'responsibilities in action' is H. Richard

Niebuhr. When he died in 1962, before completing work on a book which would have summed up his life-work on 'Christian Moral Philosophy', his son took the draft, plus the text of his lectures at Yale, and carefully built them into Niebuhr's posthumous book *The Responsible Self*.[9] The greater part of the book is in effect his lecture notes, and his son gives the reason for this:

> My father always feared that once he put his ideas into print, the possibility of reinterpreting them and rethinking them in the classroom would vanish, and instead of being a dialogue with his students, his colleagues and with the times at large his ethical reflections would become a finished piece of business, a part of the past rather than a lively, appreciative and critical response to the present.[10]

This fear of closed thinking puts him very close to Bonhoeffer, whom he met and appreciated in New York in 1939. Niebuhr did not always agree with the theological ground which supported Bonhoeffer's *Ethics*, but he would certainly have agreed with Bonhoeffer's assertion of what an ethic is not:

> An ethic cannot be a book in which there is set out how everything in the world actually ought to be but unfortunately is not, and an ethicist cannot be . . . the competent critic and judge of every human activity. An ethic cannot be a retort in which ethical or Christian human beings are produced, and the ethicist cannot be the embodiment or ideal type of a life which is, on principle, moral.[11]

Karl Barth quoted that passage with enthusiasm, and it is also quoted by James Gustafson in his Introduction to Niebuhr's *The Responsible Self* as a passage which clearly defines Niebuhr's sense of the limitation of ethics. In fact there is much in *The Responsible Self* very close to Bonhoeffer's *Ethics*, but it goes beyond it in relating to our post-war world. Niebuhr also rejects Barth's distinction between theological ethics and philosophical ethics. Neither will he accept ethics as merely self-knowledge, although he evinces a critical sympathy with such views when he approves of moving from the question 'What is real?' to 'Who am I?' He carries enough of

Calvin to insist that this kind of self-knowledge occurs for the Christian (and for any believer in God) in relation to knowledge of God. Unlike Barth, however, Niebuhr does not think that the *substance* of our self-knowledge is *derived* from our knowledge of God, but that 'Ethics is knowledge of ourselves in relation to our knowledge of God.' This is close to both Micah and James, as considered in the previous section. It is also illustrative of Bonhoeffer's point that 'thinking will be confined to your responsibilities in action'.

For Niebuhr, self-knowledge is no mere luxury to be cultivated in an idle moment; it is essential to the responsible life, it aids people in their struggle to achieve integrity. The use of ethical analysis is to help us understand ourselves as responsible beings and our world as the place where our human responsibility is exercised; and in practice it clarifies, interprets and provides a pattern of meaning and understanding in the light of which human action can be more responsible.

THE PLACE OF THE BIBLE

For centuries the Bible had in different ways provided a source-book of Christian ethics, but in the last two centuries the critical study of the Bible has gradually raised questions about its authority. More directly, the questions have been about how it has been used. Niebuhr rejects two uses:

a) the liberal use of the Bible which finds the basic foundation for Christian ethics in the teaching of Jesus;
b) the exclusively biblically based foundation of Christian ethics.

But in rejecting the first, he was led to a wider use of the Bible; while in rejecting the second, he went beyond the Bible.

Niebuhr included Bonhoeffer among those theologians whom he regarded as being too exclusively biblical. He felt that he needed to go beyond the Bible if he was to address the complexities of human responsibility. But there are indications which he does not note that Bonhoeffer was himself beginning to recognise this. There is also no doubt that Niebuhr profited from being in the freedom of the American schools rather than the Barth-dominated German theological schools. He was deeply involved in what the Bible said, but he did not feel bound to ground everything he wished to say upon it.

James Gustafson points out[12] that in his *Radical Monotheism and Western Culture* Niebuhr had already defined his framework by his strong affirmation that only the One is absolute, and all other beings, purposes, cultural expressions, politics and religion are relative to Him. With such a framework he can assert the limitations of scripture and attack narrow biblicism. For Christian ethics the Bible has an inescapable authority without being absolute. Niebuhr will not give a rank of authority to the Bible, because he rejects such hierarchical or spatial terms:

> The Church stands alongside the Bible as an authority, but it also stands under the Bible. No simple diagram of authority in Christian morals can be drawn; there is an authority of the Spirit, of immediate intuitive assurance as is claimed most forcibly by the Quakers; there is an authority of reason which is associated with our nature, and which is related to the way in which we think ethically in the face of Scripture; nature itself has a mediate authority for Christian morality – there are certain demands made by our natural social existence dealt with in terms of natural law by some theologians, and orders of creation by others. Any effort to make a permanent rank and universal rank-order of these things *a priori* distorts and finally falsifies the reality of moral existence in the Christian community.[13]

The Bible is a dependable, reliable, honest, truthful witness to the life of men before God. It can be useful, but it is variable. It has an educational authority and a corroborative authority. It is unique, both in content and in function. Niebuhr places a high value on the Bible, but he is not a biblical fundamentalist, and he believes that other sources are needed for determining the ethical attitudes of a Christian.

THE MEANING OF RESPONSIBILITY

The modern sense of the word 'responsible' is rather different from the use it once had. For a long period, including the epic periods of Bible translation, 'responsible' meant 'corresponding to'. In the nineteenth and twentieth centuries the word assumed importance as meaning three attitudes:

a) the attitude of response to an action upon us;
b) the interpretation of the action upon us, and the considered response;
c) the action taken after consideration of the reaction to be expected to our response.

Niebuhr uses this analysis to show how we may act responsibly in society. 'Our action', he writes, 'is responsible when it is response to action upon us in a continuing discourse or interaction among beings forming a continuing society . . . Personal responsibility implies the continuity of a self with a relatively consistent scheme of interpretations of what it is reacting to.'[14]

That may sound a little like what Bonhoeffer attacks as 'the luxury of the onlooker', but that would not be true. Richard Niebuhr, supporting his brother Reinhold, was able to give him his theological undergirding for his social action and follow it himself. This is a position which is much nearer to what Bonhoeffer described when he said: 'For you thought and action will enter on a new relationship; your thinking will be confined to your responsibilities in action.'[15]

Niebuhr finds support for his view of 'responsibility' as response in the Old Testament prophets, particularly Isaiah. At a critical point in Israel's history (and the same is shown to be true of the early Christian community) the decisive question is not 'What is the law?', but 'What is happening?', and then 'What is the fitting response to what is happening?' So a prophet like Isaiah does not remind the people of the law which they are required to obey, or even the goal to which they are directed, but he calls attention to what God intends, hidden within the action of Israel's enemies. This is also true of Jeremiah, who, like Micah, foretells the destruction of the

Temple and Jerusalem by the Babylonians. God's intention, hidden within the triumphant action of the Babylonians, has to be explained as 'for your sake' in order that Israel might make the appropriate response. In the same way the cross, which may be seen as the action of the enemies of the Christian church, has to be seen as God's intention hidden within the action of the enemies. The heart of the first preaching was that interpretation: 'This Jesus, delivered up according to the definite plan and foreknowledge of God, you crucified and killed by the hands of lawless men' (Acts 2:23). Much the same interpretation is found of Joseph's brethren in the Old Testament: 'And now do not be distressed, or angry with yourselves, because you sold me here; for God sent me before you to preserve life' (Genesis 45:5).

Richard Niebuhr interprets responsible action in society as the response to the other person within the community context and in the presence of God. It is a triadic form of human response. He is not alone in calling attention to the social nature of selfhood. Sociologists, cultural anthropologists and social psychologists in the 1950s and 1960s rejected the idea of society as a social contract, in which individuals entered into individual contracts with each other in order to gain limited common ends and to maintain law and order. Instead, admitting that Hobbesian contract societies still exist, they pressed for an understanding of society as face-to-face community in which unlimited commitments are the rule and where every aspect of every self's existence is conditioned by membership in the interpersonal group. The understanding of the self as social, living in response-relations to other selves, has been current in moral philosophy for centuries, but these newer disciplines have given it added force. Niebuhr builds upon this his understanding of the 'responsible self' by adding a third dimension. He draws upon Martin Buber to take the I-Thou relationship as far as he can, distinguishing it from our relationship to things – even computers. But the response of persons is not only to one another in the community context. My response to you includes also that to which we both respond. The example of nature is a fairly obvious one. Our relationship one to another is conditioned by the way we both respond to nature. But this third reality is more complex than that. In our responses to our companions, it has a double character. On the one hand it is something personal; on the other it contains within itself a reference to something that transcends it or to which it refers. Thus in civic life we educate children not only to relate to one another, but also to their history, the ideas behind those who made European civilisation what it is, their cause. Niebuhr has an important paragraph in which he relates this to the church and its reference outside itself:

> I might more readily have drawn my illustrations of the triadic situation, in which we are responsible, from the church . . . It seems evident that as I respond in the church I respond to my companions, i.e. to the fellowship of the members of the church. They have taught me the language, the words, the logic of religious discourse. But the discourse is not about them, it is about a third. To these fellow members I am challenged to be faithful, but not otherwise than in faithfulness to the common cause. That common cause is represented to me by the prophets and apostles. Yet they point beyond themselves. And even when I find that I can be responsible to the church only as I respond to Jesus Christ, I discover in him one who points beyond himself to the cause to which he is faithful and in faithfulness to which he is faithful to his companions – not the companions encountered in the church, but in the world to which the Creator is faithful, which the Creator has made his cause.[16]

This attitude to the church is consistent with Niebuhr's view that social ethics regards the present time and its given structures as the *locus* in which a person exercises his 'deputyship' under God.

DEPUTYSHIP

In that part of his *Ethics* which deals with 'The Structure of Responsible Life', Bonhoeffer has a short section on 'Deputyship'.[17] Some of the points in that section are taken up by Richard Niebuhr and developed further in his final lecture in *The Responsible Self*, which is called 'Responsibility and Christ'. Bonhoeffer, like Niebuhr, rejected the idea of the isolated individual as the subject or performer of ethical action. People act as deputies for others – the mother for her children, the teacher for his or her pupils, the statesman for his country. Even though Jesus was not married, and did not have a profession, he is not outside the field of responsibility. His deputyship is for all people.[18] As Bonhoeffer develops that idea we see how near he is to what I have quoted above from Richard Niebuhr. Bonhoeffer writes in his unfinished *Ethics*:

> Responsibility, as life and action in deputyship, is essentially a relation of man to man. Christ became man and He thereby bore responsibility and deputyship for men. There is also a responsibility for things, conditions and values . . . Through Christ the world of things and of values is once more directed towards mankind as it was in the Creation.[19]

Both Bonhoeffer and Niebuhr make a clear distinction between concrete ethical decisions and theories of ethics. Decisions have an exclusive validity. Once we have decided that a certain act is right or wrong, we must proceed and accept the consequences for ourselves. An ethical theory is quite different, we commit ourselves to it only tentatively. No theory can be exclusive, it remains a way of understanding our life in terms of responsibility.

With that warning not to take our theories too seriously, or to make them absolute, Niebuhr proceeds to develop from Bonhoeffer's 'Responsibility as life in deputyship' a Christian ethos which is exemplified by Christ, an ethics of 'universal responsibility'. It is to be found in other religions and other philosophies, and for Christians it is uniquely demonstrated in the life and teaching of Jesus. Basically, it is to interpret every particular event as included in universal action. This is the ethos of citizenship in a universal society, in which no being that exists and no action that takes place can be interpreted outside the universal context. It is also the ethics of eternal life, in the sense that no act of any person which is in response to action upon that person can fail to involve repercussions, reactions, extending towards infinity in time and space.

The implications of that for the unknown martyr are considerable. The victim in Hitler's death camp at Auschwitz or Belsen was told on entry that he would not get out alive and that no one would ever know what happened to him or her. The silence of eternity was the lie that was intended to break the spirit. It is not surprising that Jews have since those awful days pathologically feared that the Holocaust might be forgotten. They have recognised their deputyship for those who died and no one knew.

Niebuhr insists that the ethos of universal responsibility is not uniquely Christian, and he is able to show how potent it is in the Old Testament. It is significant that Christians turn to the Old Testament more often than the New for their guidance in social ethics. It is the prophets rather than the apostles who provide the basis for social protest and demands for justice. The whole ethos of the Old Testament is responsibility to the one and universal God. Again, the Joseph story provides a good example of this. When Joseph says to his brothers: 'You meant evil against me; but God meant it for good, to bring it about that many people should be kept alive' (Genesis 50:20), he makes a clear distinction between the particular intention that guides a specific action and the divine intention that uses and lies behind the action. There is no legalism in that kind of thinking, but rather interpretation and response.

A further example of this can be found in Isaiah 10. The question is how to meet an emergency – the invasion of the land by a hostile power. The prophet answers the question 'What shall we do?' by interpreting the situation. The invasion is to be understood as an act of God; the question to ask is 'What is God doing?' The prophet explains that God is purging his people, and therefore the invasion must not be explained as the attack of the ungodly upon the godly. The destructive intention of the Assyrians is one thing – they are godless too, as indeed Israel is by her disobedience – but the holy, saving intention of God is another. Then comes the answer to the question 'What are we to do?' It is not that they should pray to God to deliver them from the ungodly invader, asking God to save his people. No. It is a call for internal reformation. The defence against Assyria is secondary. This tenth chapter of Isaiah is a good example of Hebrew ethics on which Christians draw. Of course they read it as Christians, but they also know that they are indebted to the Jews. In fact we understand our Christ with the aid of Hebrew scriptures.

Jew and Stoic alike help us to see the wide variety of influences that have determined our attitude to universal responsibility and show us our interdependence with others, persons and things, the human community and nature. Not all our ethics come uniquely from Christ. We have learnt responsibility to God in all our reactions to actions upon us – as Christ did in his incarnate life. But we see Christ in a double role. He is symbol of all that we have learnt from other sources, demonstrating in his earthly life total responsibility and obedience to God. But he is also the one who accomplishes reconciliation with God. Our theories of the atonement are always inadequate, but the fact remains that the movement from obedient resignation to reconciliation is the movement inaugurated by Jesus Christ. Let me end this section with a further quotation from Richard Niebuhr, who seems to follow Bonhoeffer in this development of responsibility more fruitfully than any other theologian of the 1960s:

> By Jesus Christ men have been and are empowered to become sons of God – not as those who have been saved out of a perishing world but as those who know that the world is being saved. That its being saved from destruction involves the burning up of an infinite amount of tawdry human works, that it involves the healing of a miasmic ocean of disease, the resurrection of the dead, the forgiveness of sins, the making good of an infinite number of irresponsibilities, that such making good is not done except by suffering servants who often do not know the name of Christ though they bear his image – all this Christians know. Nevertheless, they move toward their end and all endings as those who, knowing defeats, do not believe in defeat.[20]

In this there is no place for boasting. We have no superior way of life to show to others. We are often shamed by those who do not acknowledge the name of Christ. We who are Christians can only say that once we were blind and now we begin to see; we were aliens and now we begin to feel at home; we were in love with ourselves and our little cities and now we are falling in love with the city of God, the universal community of which God is the source and governor. And for all this we are indebted to Jesus Christ, in our history, and in the depth of the spirit in which we grope with our theologies and symbols.

'BUT THE SPIRITUAL FORCE IS LACKING'

At about the time when Bonhoeffer was working on his book, of which he left only an outline and many letters, Eberhard Bethge was also writing. The comments that Bonhoeffer makes on his 'couple of closely packed pages'[21] help us to see how he would have proceeded, if he had been given time and strength to do so. He congratulates Bethge with great warmth, amazed at his friend's achievement, particularly commending his simplicity, which he describes as 'an intellectual achievement, one of the greatest'.[22] Bethge had admitted that he had to wrestle hard for that simplicity.

Then Bonhoeffer shows the contrast between the two and their need for each other:

> I believe that with a sure touch you've found the appropriate form for yourself – narrative, first person – and the right subject-matter – what you yourself have experienced, seen, observed, been through, felt, thought. Your gift of *seeing* seems to me to be the most important thing. And precisely *how* and *what* you see. This is no urgent, analytical, curious seeing, that wants to pry into everything, but clear, open and reverent seeing. *This* kind of seeing, with which I'm concerned in the problems of theology – *theoretically* – is now leading you to . . . descriptive writing. I think that here perhaps our strong spiritual affinity – with me it's a matter of seeing with the intellect, whereas you use your eyes and all your senses, but the manner of seeing is related – or the most important result of our long spiritual fellowship is to be found . . .[23]

The letter is not complete, but one thing is clear, that Bonhoeffer saw Eberhard Bethge as complementing his own view of things. The two together constitute a spiritual whole. This is what gives a superior quality to Bethge's monumental biography.[24] It is Bonhoeffer with all his restless intellectual curiosity and courage, recounted with Bethge's power of observation and total commitment to life – although he does not lack intellectual curiosity either. But what Bonhoeffer praises his writing for is his observation with his whole self. Although any reader of that biography gets the impression that it is Bonhoeffer who has the total approach to life – 'eyes and all your senses'!

If we continue Bonhoeffer's thought we shall have to include both elements: the theoretical, seeing with the intellect, and the open and reverent seeing. With the intellect alone the spiritual force is lacking. Bonhoeffer has no doubt about that when he looks at the state of the church to which he belonged. Its theology had failed it in the hour of trial. If he had lived, his experience would not have encouraged him at first. The German Protestant churches after the war did their best to get back to where they were. Karl Barth in Switzerland, with great influence over the Confessing Church in Germany, showed no interest in re-establishing the institutions of the German churches, but believed that the whole tone of the 'new' church must be set by the Confessing Church, which had maintained its integrity. He thought that the Barmen Declaration should be the charter of the post-war church. But he did not command majority opinion. The churches like Bavaria and Hanover described themselves as 'intact' churches and were anxious to get back to normal after purging away some Nazi and German Christian elements. The Confessing Church, of course, had great influence in such areas as the Rhineland, Westphalia and Prussia, but the influence was not strong enough to prevent a gradual slip back into the old patterns. An interesting example of this was the question of the church tax which financed the work of the church. A World Council of Churches report after a visit to Berlin had the following paragraph:

> The *Bekennende Kirche* [*i.e.* the Confessing Church] told the State more than once that it would gladly renounce all subsidies in exchange for freedom to preach according to its conscience and

to fill its own offices itself. The Church still entertains this desire to finance itself solely from offerings and collections without aid from the State. However during this transitional period the church would not be able to make ends meet, having lost all resources twice in twenty-five years.[25]

The church tax was restored and continues to this day.

But there are signs of renewal. From that same report comes the transcript of what Bishop Dibelius, as President of the Oberkirchenrat, sent to all officials and employees of the church:

> Genuine church authorities must know how to repent. Therefore I say openly that those church officials bear an enormous guilt, who in the last ten years permitted themselves to become the instruments of unchristian ambition instead of defending the cause of Christ in courageous faith against the National Socialist State. This guilt must be acknowledged and expiated. It is part of this expiation that those who were responsible for the disastrous behaviour of the Old Prussian Church authorities must leave the ecclesiastical administration. The Church which struggles for a renewal within must also have an inwardly renewed administration.[26]

Martin Niemöller, disappointed that the Confessing Church was not organised to fulfil its post-war role, appealed for a Declaration of Guilt and obtained it at Stuttgart.

These are a few of the observed examples that gave no clear message to the future. A new task was needed, which was not the restoration of the situation which failed, both in Germany and throughout Christendom. The conclusion of any observer in 1945 would have been 'the spiritual force is lacking'.

But that was not the whole picture. The World Council of Churches, still in process of formation, sent representatives to Germany as soon as hostilities ceased. Stewart Herman, an American Lutheran pastor, formerly serving in Berlin, was the principal representative who visited in the earliest possible days after the war. He sent copious reports,[27] and the world churches were soon informed. They were present at the Council of the Evangelical Church in Germany on 18 and 19 October 1945 in Stuttgart. They had not demanded a confession of guilt, but their presence enabled the German churches

to subscribe to a Confession which sent a new wave of
spiritual power through the country. It was signed by those
who had resisted the excesses of National Socialism, suffering
imprisonment and persecution. Yet they identified themselves with their more obviously guilty brothers and sisters.
The Confession of Guilt[28] read:

> We are not only conscious of oneness with our nation in a great
> community of suffering, but also in a solidarity of guilt. With
> great pain we say: Unending suffering has been brought by us to
> many peoples and countries. That which we have often witnessed
> to our congregations we now proclaim in the name of the whole
> church: We have in fact fought for long years in the name of Jesus
> Christ against the spirit which found its terrible expression in the
> National Socialist government by force; but we accuse ourselves
> that we did not witness more courageously, pray more faithfully,
> believe more joyously, love more ardently.

The statement continued with a hope of a new beginning,
united with the churches of the ecumenical fellowship:

> We hope in God that through the joint service of the churches,
> the spirit of violence and revenge, that begins today again to
> become powerful, may be controlled, and the spirit of peace and
> love come to command (the spirit) in which alone tortured
> humanity can find healing.
> So we pray in a time when the whole world needs a new
> beginning:
> *Veni creator spiritus!*

This was the new beginning that Bonhoeffer had hoped for.
Many years earlier, probably in 1940, he had written that part
of his *Ethics* which he called, 'The Confession of Guilt'.[29] In it
he writes:

> The Church confesses that she has witnessed the lawless applica-
> tion of brutal force, the physical and spiritual suffering of count-
> less innocent people, oppression, hatred and murder, and that
> she has not raised her voice on behalf of the victims and has
> not found ways to hasten to their aid. She is guilty of the
> deaths of the weakest and most defenceless brothers of Jesus
> Christ.[30]

But what Bonhoeffer was talking about was something far more radical than this Stuttgart Declaration. He required a confession of guilt which was understood in Christ:

> The only way to turn back is through recognition of the guilt incurred towards Christ . . . By her confession of guilt [in this way] the Church does not exempt men from their own confession of guilt, but she calls them in into the fellowship of the confession of guilt. Apostate humanity can endure before Christ only if it has fallen under the sentence of Christ. It is to this judgement that the Church summons all those who hear her message.[31]

The Stuttgart Declaration was very far from this. It was almost – although not explicitly – demanded by the representatives of the World Council, it was not spontaneous and it had taken a long time. The confession came only after the total collapse of Germany and in the face of the bitterness, indignation and contempt that rained upon them from every side. One should not disclaim the value of this unique declaration, unprecedented in the history of Protestant Christianity in Germany. But it did not renew the nation. It was left to the industrialists and economists to perform what was called the 'German miracle'.

Far nearer to Bonhoeffer's call for a confession of guilt, but on much too small a scale, was the action of Director Hildemann of Tutzing Evangelical Academy. When the war was over he called together those young men who had been Nazis and asked them: 'Where did the church fail you?'

We have already noted Bonhoeffer's deep sense of guilt and his solidarity with the guilty in his poem 'Night Voices in Tegel'. Keith Clements has also pointed to this in the 'fictional writings' in prison.[32] If we put all this together with the section already referred to in the *Ethics* on guilt, we have a theological structure based upon Bonhoeffer's Christology.

A confession of guilt in 1940, when Germany was winning the war, is very different from a confession of guilt in 1945 when the war was already lost and Germany was at the mercy of her conquerors. Bonhoeffer anticipated the excuses – there was nothing we could do, we were hemmed in on every side, it is not the church which is guilty but the others – but, he writes:

This is the voice of unbelief, which sees in the confession of guilt only a dangerous moral derogation and which fails to see that the confession of guilt is the re-attainment of the form of Jesus Christ who bore the sin of the world. For indeed the free confession of guilt is not something which can be done or left undone at will. It is the emergence of the form of Jesus Christ in the Church. Either the Church must willingly undergo this transformation, or else she must cease to be the Church of Christ.[33]

The full meaning of that was not understood at Stuttgart, and the formal confession was too late and not profound enough.

3

THE SUFFERING OF GOD IN A
GODLESS WORLD

Religion is a foreboding word, threatening and promising at the same time. It tells of rules and regulations which must be kept and of a God who acts justly, rewarding and punishing according to the way in which the rules and regulations are kept or not. The word means, literally, 'binding back'. It is derived from two Latin parts: *ligo* – to bind; *re* – back. It is a word of 'restraint'. In most religions the restraint is on both God and man. When the rules are properly kept, the God is obliged to perform. A more sophisticated attitude to God develops in the higher religions, but the word keeps its basic meaning of 'restraint'. The word 'religion' is not used in the Old Testament and seldom in the New. The usage in the New Testament is largely critical, attacking certain elements in current Judaism as 'the Jews' religion'. The only exception is the verse in James, already quoted, which defines a 'true religion', as distinct, presumably, from religions of rules and regulations, such as the pagans practised.

Christianity is in this sense a break away from religion, not to a godless philosophy, but to a different relationship with God, already beginning in the later prophets of the Old Testament. Bonhoeffer encapsulates this change in a short poem entitled 'Christians and Pagans'.[1] The first stanza defines the natural approach to the all-powerful God, of weak humans seeking help in their distress. Christians also do this.

> Men go to God when they are sore bestead,
> Pray to him for succour, for his peace, for bread,
> For mercy for them sick, sinning, or dead;
> All men do so, Christian and unbelieving.

The second stanza defines the relationship of Christians to a suffering God. The suffering and death of Jesus, his weakness before the powers of this world, is more than an example for Christians to imitate. It is an understanding of God who is incarnate in the man Jesus, suffering, weak, vulnerable. The Old Testament has a picture of God's chosen servant (presumably his people) suffering; reversing the accepted views of privilege. God's people are to be a blessing, to bring light to a world of darkness, not by conquest, but by suffering. In Gethsemane and on the cross, the Christian recognises the incarnate God, suffering for the sins of the world. You do not pray to the crucified God for victory, he commands no legions to rescue him. He is God forsaken, not triumphant. Christians stand by him or they fall. The sleeping disciples in Gethsemane are still trusting his protection as in the storm on the lake. Jesus pleads with them for help: 'Could you not watch one little hour with me?' God seeks help from his followers in his hour of distress:

> Men go to God when he is sore bestead,
> Find him poor and scorned, without shelter or bread,
> Whelmed under weight of the wicked, the weak, the dead;
> Christians stand by God in his hour of grieving.

The distinction between pagan and Christian lies in their attitude to God, not in his attitude to them. In the traditional words 'Christ died for the sins of the world', Bonhoeffer had found already new and revolutionary meaning. As a pietistic statement, it is no more than saying that the gospel should be preached to every creature and the offer to salvation be made. In this poem, he portrays God as 'saving the world', not rescuing Christians out of it. The suffering God forgives and succours Christian and pagan alike. The simple statement of Jesus that God's rain falls on the just and the unjust is taken to the limit of universal forgiveness:

> God goes to every man when sore bestead,
> Feeds body and spirit with his bread;
> For Christians, pagans alike he hangs dead,
> And both alike forgiving.

With this approach of God to man, Bonhoeffer has left us with a dilemma, but it is a biblical one. The false picture of 'God' as a working hypothesis, 'as a stop-gap for our embarrassments', has become superfluous by the development of man's control over his world. It is not man in his weakness who needs to meet with God, but man at his strongest point, when he is successful. It is when he (or she) has mastered the menace of nature by superior technology, provided food and housing for dependents, is fulfilled and has handled life adequately with all its problems, perhaps with the help of the sciences of medicine and psychotherapy – then he or she needs forgiveness. And that is not because some secret fault has been found. (How the gutter press enjoys uncovering the secret vices of the virtuous public figure!) That is not what Bonhoeffer means by the need for forgiveness. He does not receive that forgiveness from a God who is successful and powerful, all-wise and competent, an image of himself. Such a God he does not need – a superfluous working hypothesis. Yet, the God who has allowed him to live in the world without this working hypothesis is the God before whom he stands continually. As Bonhoeffer said in that crucial letter of 16 July 1944, 'Before God and with God we live without God.'[2] This is not to reject the God of creation or to adopt an image of God as the clockmaker who put the universe together and then left it to run, with the growing competence of man to handle breakdowns. God is still there. He has allowed himself to be pushed out of the world only 'on to the cross'. That means that his power is not used to sustain the successful in their success. He is weak and powerless in the world: 'He took our infirmities, and bore our diseases'. God in Christ helps us by his weakness and suffering. But he helps all men and women, not simply Christians.

> For Christians, pagans alike he hangs dead,
> And both alike forgiving.

THE DILEMMA OF DISTINCTION

It is impossible to escape the division which permeates the gospel message and the parables of Jesus. There are children of light and children of darkness; there are wise virgins and foolish virgins; there are wheat and tares; there are the similes of houses built on rock and those on sand. Such divisions have been used in evangelical preaching to signify those who accept Christ and those who refuse him. They give an edge to the preaching of the gospel – repent and be saved, or refuse and be damned! There is a great deal in the New Testament to support this simplistic preaching, but it does not conform with the view of the compassionate God presented in the Bible.

Certainly in the Old Testament, God is portrayed as setting down the conditions under which he will protect his people. The prophets constantly warn Israel that her disobedience will lead to rejection. Yet as early as the eighth century BC Hosea declares that God will not give her up. As late as the fifth century BC Jeremiah admits that the covenant lies shattered and God should walk away from it. The fires that blaze over a conquered Jerusalem tell of Israel's doom. But God has not delivered them over to the Babylonians; he has himself destroyed Jerusalem because it was a hindrance to their relationship with him. He is already fashioning a different kind of covenant. He is seeking a direct relationship, person to person, in which goodness comes from the heart rather than the law courts. This is not the kind of God who would damn for eternity those who could neither understand nor accept the doctrine of the atonement. Certainly, John the Baptist comes with a divisive message; but it is not intended to divide. It is intended to prepare. Repentance is at its heart. Jerusalem and all Judaea come out to meet him, but he offers no privileged seats in heaven – only a way to prepare for the coming of God's Messiah. And the divisions of the gospel parables are also about preparation for meeting the returning Christ. And none of them stresses the acceptance of Christian teaching or even conversion. They all talk about watchfulness, being ready.

Matthew gives his warning twice. It occurs first in his

summary of the teaching of Jesus in what we call 'The Sermon on the Mount' (Matthew 5–7), which he ends with a parable of division – the houses built on rock and sand. The differences has nothing to do with religious belief: 'Every one then who hears these words of mine and does them will be like a wise man who built his house upon the rock' (Matthew 7:24). Alternatively, 'every one who hears these words of mine and does not do them will be like a foolish man who built his house upon the sand' (Matthew 7:26). The difference lies in putting into practice what we have heard and know to be the true way. The criterion applies to Christians and pagans alike. Before using this parable, Matthew tells of Jesus comparing life to a fruit tree. The criterion is the nature of the fruit – good or bad, not orthodox or heretic. To reinforce that point he says: 'Not every one who says to me, "Lord, Lord," shall enter the kingdom of heaven, but he who does the will of my Father who is in heaven' (Matthew 7:21). And in case we have put a religious interpretation upon those lines: 'On that day many will say to me, "Lord, Lord, did we not prophesy in your name, and cast out demons in your name, and do many mighty works in your name?"' (Matthew 7:22). These surely are proved to be Christian because they demonstrate the power of the Spirit. They are true charismatics! Yet Jesus the Good Shepherd who knows his sheep does not know them. They are 'evildoers' and are sent away. In greater detail and in the same gospel, Matthew records the parable of the last judgement. There a new element is introduced. Obedience to the Father is shown as care for the other, and it is identified with care for the suffering Christ. This is not the imitation of Christ, it is the identifying of Christ in the distress of the other. The account begins with all the splendour of Jewish eschatological writing:

> When the Son of man comes in his glory, and all the angels with him, then he will sit on his glorious throne. Before him will be gathered all the nations, and he will separate them one from another as a shepherd separates the sheep from the goats . . . (Matthew 25:31)

This is not Jesus abandoned, but in glory. He is a judge, determining who is to enjoy the inheritance of his Father's kingdom. The division is between the righteous and those who are cursed. Strong language. But two things stand out – the criteria of judgement and the surprise of all concerned that they are placed where they are. Both righteous and cursed are expecting something different. The criteria are entirely concerned with caring for those in distress:

> for I was hungry and you gave me food, I was thirsty and you gave me drink, I was a stranger and you welcomed me, I was naked and you clothed me, I was sick and you visited me, I was in prison and you came to me. (Matthew 25:35–36)

The righteous had done these things, but were surprised to hear that it had anything to do with Jesus, the Son of Man; the cursed were equally surprised because they would certainly have done all those things to Jesus, if he had need, but did not realise that he was there, lurking in the hungry, the thirsty, the naked, the stranger, the sick and the prisoner.

This is not another form of justification by works rather than by faith. It is the identifying of Christ and our service to him. It is also a shattering view of the criteria of choice for the kingdom of God.

The identifying of Christ with the distressed, or 'the poor', is what lifts this teaching of the criteria above mere humanitarianism. The righteous do not care for the poor because they *see* Christ in them, but they are serving Christ because he has *identified* himself with the poor. That is what the line

> Christians stand by God in his hour of grieving

really means.

SHARING IN GOD'S SUFFERING

'Man is summoned to share in God's sufferings at the hands of a godless world.'[3]

Once we have torn ourselves away from fear of heresy in thinking of a God who suffers, we are able to see the agony of God in a world that inflicts inhuman cruelty upon people. God's sorrow is not that the world is irreligious, but that it is inhuman.

In her perceptive novel *Peter Abelard*, Helen Waddell has a scene towards the end when the cruelly treated Abelard is with his faithful friend Thibault. They are about to eat a late supper when they hear a cry that sounds like that of a child. They run to find out, and discover a rabbit caught in a trap and dying in pain. Peter Abelard takes the rabbit out of the trap and it dies in his hands:

It lay for a moment breathing quickly, then in some blind recognition of the kindness that had met it at the last, the small head thrust and nestled against his arm, and it died.

It was that last confiding thrust that broke Abelard's heart. He looked down at the little draggled body, his mouth shaking. 'Thibault,' he said, 'do you think there is a God at all? Whatever has come to me, I earned it. But what did this one do?'

Thibault nodded.

'I know,' he said. 'Only – I think God is in it too.'

Abelard looked up sharply.

'In it? Do you mean that it makes Him suffer, the way it does us?'

Again Thibault nodded.

'Then why doesn't he stop it?'

'I don't know,' said Thibault, 'Unless – unless it's like the Prodigal Son. I suppose the father could have kept him at home against his will. But what would have been the use? All this,' he stroked the limp body, 'is because of us. But all the time God suffers. More than we do.'

Abelard looked at him, perplexed.

'Thibault, when did you think of all this?'

Thibault's face stiffened. 'It was that night,' he said, his voice strangled. 'The things we did to – to poor Guibert. He –' Thibault stopped. 'I could not sleep for nights and nights. And then I saw that God suffered too. And I thought I would like to be a priest.'

'Thibault, do you mean Calvary?'

Thibault shook his head. 'That was only a piece of it – the piece that we saw – in time. Like that.' He pointed to a fallen tree beside them, sawn through the middle. 'That dark ring there, it goes up and down the whole length of the tree. But you only see it where it is cut across. That is what Christ's life was; the bit of God that we saw. And we think God is like that, because Christ was like that, kind, and forgiving sins and healing people. We think God is like that for ever, because it happened once, with Christ.

But not the pain. Not the agony at the last. We think that
stopped.'
    Abelard looked at him, the blunt nose and the wide mouth, the
honest troubled eyes. He could have knelt before him.
    'Then, Thibault,' he said slowly, 'you think that all this,' he
looked down at the little quiet body in his arms, 'all the pain of the
world, was Christ's cross?'
    'God's cross,' said Thibault. 'And it goes on.'
    'The Patripassian heresy,' murmured Abelard mechanically.
'But, O God, if it were true. Thibault, it must be. At least, there is
something at the back of it that is true. And if we could find it – it
would bring back the whole world.'
    'I couldn't ever rightly explain it,' said Thibault. 'But you
could, if you would think it out.' He reached out his hand, and
stroked the long ears. 'Old lop-ears,' he said. 'Maybe this is why
he died. Come and have your supper, Master Peter. We'll bury
him somewhere near the oratory. In holy ground.'[4]

I have long regarded that passage as a very fine piece of
theological writing. That novel was first published in 1933. It
was set in that period of European history which Bonhoeffer
saw as the beginning of the coming of age of humanity. Helen
Waddell rightly retains the 'religious' framework of the
period, but Abelard, perhaps a little before his time, is
seeking a liberation from religious servitude.

The Renaissance has happened since then, and we as
Christians can recognise a pioneer of modern thought. There
is a sense of liberation in being set free from false religious
obligations and inhibitions. We can see that being a Christian
does not mean being a particular kind of religious person. It
means being human, participating in the sufferings of God in
the contemporary world, allowing oneself to be caught up
into the way of Jesus Christ, into the messianic event. The
best description of that is still Isaiah 53.

In the New Testament it is described in many different
ways. There is first of all the call to discipleship. What kind of
disciples does Jesus call? We need to step back from the
traditional language of the gospels, which over the centuries
has acquired a religious flavour, to grasp the extraordinary
nature of this call. Bonhoeffer in his book *The Cost of
Discipleship*, which came out of his lectures at Finkenwalde,

already showed his grasp of the nature of Christ's call.[5] In his letter of 18 July 1944 he says of the call in the New Testament that it appears

> in Jesus' table-fellowship with sinners, in 'conversions' in the narrower sense of the word (e.g. Zacchaeus), in the act of the woman who was a sinner (Luke 7) – an act that she performed without any confession of sin, in the healing of the sick . . . in Jesus' acceptance of children. The shepherds, like the wise men from the East, stand at the crib, not as 'converted sinners', but simply because they are drawn to the crib by the star just as they are. The centurion of Capernaum (who makes no confession of sin) is held up as a model of faith (cf. Jairus). Jesus 'loved' the rich young man. The eunuch (Acts 8) and Cornelius (Acts 10) are not standing at the edge of an abyss. Nathaniel is 'an Israelite indeed, in whom there is no guile' (John I.47). Finally, Joseph of Arimathea and the women at the tomb. The only thing that is common to all these is their sharing in the suffering of God in Christ. That is their 'faith'. There is nothing of religious method here.[6]

Bonhoeffer adds that the religious act is always something partial, but faith is something whole. 'Jesus calls men, not to a new religion, but to life.'[7]

A COVENANT WITH LIFE

One of the most perceptive attempts to recover the impact of Jesus upon his generation was published in German in 1986 and translated the following year by John Bowden as *The Shadow of the Galilean* by Gerd Theissen (London: SCM Press).

Described as 'The Quest of the Historical Jesus in Narrative Form', it is well researched and lively reading. Jesus does not appear, only his influence. We read of him as others saw him and were disturbed by him. The principal character, Andreas, sets out to discover all he can about Jesus. At last, he sees him dying on a cross. After that, in high fever, Andreas dreams a frightening dream of beasts taking over the earth. At last he awakes and is convinced of the power of this

Jesus, dead though he be, and cannot put into words what he
believes. Gerd Theissen's words describe his state as Andreas
sees the risen Jesus, a figure with a human form, emitting a
warm light and releasing him from the terror of his dreams:

> It was Jesus, a changed Jesus. I had only seen him once – from the
> city wall of Jerusalem. At that time he was hanging dead on a
> cross, but now he radiated life, peace and freedom. The rule of
> the beasts was at an end. I woke up, happy but confused.
>
> I got up from my bed, went out into the open air and looked at
> the sea from the upper storey of our house. Behind a white strip
> of sand increasingly deep darkness spread westwards, that dark-
> ness from which my confused dreams had arisen. Now it lay calm
> and still. No monster was creeping to land. No storm was
> disturbing the surface of the sea. No thunder burst against the
> shore. Something else happened. From the land the light grew
> more intense. Where sky and sea had merged, pale strips
> appeared on the horizon, coloured shadows met the invisible sun
> in the east. Rays broke out from the depths of the land. Then the
> sun appeared over the hills and covered the sea with glowing
> light. The city shyly reflected the first brightness. The buildings
> emerged increasingly clearly from the shadow of the streets.
> Temple and synagogue, the houses of Jews and Gentiles, all were
> bathed in the dawning light. The sun arose on good and evil, just
> and unjust. I felt it, bright and warm.
>
> The chaotic monsters of the night had been overcome. My
> anguish at the harshness of life was over. In me the rule of the
> beasts had come to an end. The true man had appeared to me.
> And I had recognized the features of Jesus in him. He had given
> me back the earth. It had not got better since the previous
> day. Today, as yesterday, the struggle for a chance to live
> would continue. But that wasn't everything. This battle need not
> dominate all my action and thought. I made a new covenant with
> life.
>
> I could clearly feel a voice coming to me from all things, a voice
> which offered me this covenant with life. Never again would I
> wish the earth away, never again deny life. Never again would I
> allow myself to be overcome by beasts from the abyss. I heard the
> voice, and it was one with the voice of Jesus. I had the certainty
> that wherever I went it would always accompany me. I could not
> escape it anywhere. And I responded and prayed . . .
>
> For a long time I stood like this on our house and let the dream
> of the man echo in me. The rule of the beasts could not last

forever. Some time the man had to appear, the true man. And everyone would recognize in him the features of Jesus.

Then I went to the downstairs room and woke Baruch. We ate breakfast, shared the bread, drank from the same cup and rejoiced at being together.[8]

4

THE CHURCH ON THE DEFENSIVE

We must begin with the Protestant churches of Germany. The Reformation had left them closely related to the rulers of the German states and, although the period of four centuries that followed up to the First World War had brought many changes, the basic relationship of church and ruler survived. When the Kaiser abdicated, he left the churches fatherless. The revolution that followed produced the Weimar Republic, and it separated church and state. The church, or rather churches, had to find a role.

There was little uniformity. The Reformation had produced two kinds of Protestant church, Lutheran and Reformed. The state in Prussia had blended these into a United Church, in 1817. Germany was thus divided, like a patchwork quilt, into Catholic, Lutheran, Reformed and United. There had been a steady coming together of the Protestant churches under Prussian leadership and the figure of the Kaiser. When the Kaiser abdicated on 9 November 1918, the pattern fell apart. The churches of separate provinces acquired more autonomy, and the separation of church and state left each province its own problem. This legacy became important as different churches later reacted to the Third Reich and the whirlwind of National Socialism. The Catholics of course remained more centralised, despite the separation of church and state.

An example of the way in which the churches found their role may be taken from Prussia, and in particular the writing of Otto Dibelius, the youngest superintendent in the Prussian church in 1925. He was forty-five and his influential book was called *Das Jahrhundert der Kirche* ('The Century of the Church').[1] He was able, a born church statesman, full of courage, decisiveness and independence of judgement. He had no doubt that the new situation gave the Protestant church its greatest opportunity. The new religionless state, he maintained, no longer recognised moral standards. Therefore he wrote:

> Truly it is high time that someone seized the helm with a strong hand, applied the criterion of an absolute morality to the new conditions and restored humanity to an awareness of what is good and what is evil. Who is to instil this new moral judgment? Who can do it if the church does not?[2]

Dibelius spread his canvas wide as he commented upon the current 'cult of the body', 'the pursuit of eternal youth', family planning and divorce, the meaning of punishment, gambling, luxury. He asked about the limitation of profits, the balance of rights of capital and rights of labour. The church was to shape the pattern of evangelical life in Germany.

The book was a mixed bag. There was much modern social and ethical concern, but a great deal of conservatism in the solution of the problems. The book was, however, widely read and influential. The churches saw themselves as the moral guarantors of society. And for a while it worked. Conditions improved and the independent provincial churches won through. Far fewer people left the churches than had been feared. One of the clearest statements of how the Protestant church saw its task in those days was a statement of the *Kirchenbund* (a federation of the separate *Landeskirchen*) in 1921: 'The purpose of the German *Evangelische Kirchenbund* is . . . to cultivate the collective consciousness of German Protestantism and to mobilize the concentrated forces of the German churches of the Reformation.'[3]

KARL BARTH: THE SHIFT FROM CHRISTIANS TO CHRIST

It all began in Germany with a quite unimportant conference in the village of Tambach in Thuringia. About a hundred Christians who were dissatisfied by the line their churches were taking had heard of a vigorous Christian Socialist movement in Switzerland. They invited two leaders of the movement, Kutter and Ragaz. Neither was interested. Instead a young Swiss pastor of thirty-three appeared in Tambach on 25 September 1919. He was completely unknown in Germany and did not want to give them what they wanted. He used the occasion to express for the first time a type of theology which was later to play so vital a role in the battle against National Socialism. Karl Barth was right in assuming that what they wanted was 'a sharp rejection of the capitalist economic and social order . . . an urgent challenge to support vigorously the coming new socialist order'. He was asked to speak on 'The Christian's Place in Society', and from the first word he anticipated the Barthian theology, as he interpreted his theme:

> '*The Christian*: we must be agreed that we do not mean *the Christians*, not the multitude of the baptized, nor the chosen few who are Religious Socialists, nor even the cream of the noblest and most devoted Christians we might think of. The Christian is *the Christ*.

In one phrase he had shifted theology from humanity to God, the God revealed in Jesus Christ, the God of the cross and resurrection, in all the strangeness with which he confronts the world. It is misguided to try to claim Christianity for society – whether conservative, liberal or religious. He spoke of a movement from above, 'which has neither its origin nor its aim in space, in time, or in the contingency of things . . . [it is a movement] whose power and import are revealed in the resurrection of Jesus Christ from the dead.[4] Humans close their mind to this movement, vertically from above. They do it by means of religion, Christianity and morality. Barth wanted to speak of God, not religion. He spoke of the God who says the radical *No* to all human society, and then develops from it a *Yes* to this very activity, and again transcending this *Yes* with a great *No* in order to develop another *Yes* from this *No*. At Tambach the *No* seemed louder than the *Yes*.

Nothing much came of Tambach, but six months later Karl Barth was speaking again, and this time he was addressing the question of how you can speak of God in this way in the twentieth century. The basic question was the status of the Bible. Centuries of biblical criticism had left scholars with some uncertainty in using it as an authority. Barth did not dismiss biblical criticism. He was no fundamentalist, but he found a new kind of authority in the Bible and was able to use it, and to speak of God with confidence. Revelation was a real element in Jewish and Christian faith. God had made known his ways, not through the infallible book, but through writers who responded to his revelation and in their own fallible way bore witness to the revelation of God. It was at Aarau in Switzerland on 17 April 1920 that he said this most clearly:

> We all know the curiosity that comes over us when from a window we see the people in the street suddenly stop and look up – shade their eyes with their hands and look straight up into the sky toward something which is hidden from us by the roof. Our curiosity is superfluous, for what they see is doubtless an aeroplane. But as to the sudden stopping, looking up, and tense attention characteristic of the people of the Bible, our wonder will not be so lightly dismissed. To me personally it came first with Paul: this man evidently sees and hears something which is above everything, which is absolutely beyond the range of my observation and the measure of my thought.[5]

There are many such witnesses in the Bible, but the image is always the same: 'always there is the same seeing of the invisible, the same hearing of the inaudible, the same incomprehensible but no less undeniable epidemic of standing still and looking up.[6] The Bible remained central for Barthian thought – not as religious history, not even as the source of Christian doctrine, but as a witness to an encounter. That encounter was with something that lay beyond all human thought, beyond the fears and hopes of humanity. It was objective – the Word of God.

Barth was able to bridge the gap between fundamentalists and liberals. The one regarded the Bible as 'holy and infallible', the other regarded it as an historical document which needed the criteria of historical criticism. For Karl Barth, the Bible was the witness of an encounter with God, initiated on God's side.

In that same Aarau lecture, Barth went on from his biblical line to attack 'religion' as a mere substitute for the real encounter:

> [Religion] is not satisfied with hinting at the x [unknown quantity] that is over the world *and* herself. She acts in her lofty ecclesiastical estate as if she were in possession of a gold mine; and in the so-called 'religious values' she actually pretends to give out clinking coins.[7]

Barth developed a special relationship to the world which became of vital importance in dealing later with those attracted by National Socialism. The Word of God in the Bible is directed not against the godless world, but against the *religious* world, whether it worships under the auspices of Baal or Jehovah. Barth does not lament the evil world, but argues that God, who is trivialised in religion, must be taken seriously.

His early interest in socialism continued, but more and more his theological emphasis was directed towards the church rather than society. He was politically involved, but not a political theologian. He gave the church an instrument by which to cleanse itself, and years later he would virtually write the Barmen Declaration, without any reference to the Jews. His eye was on what God was saying to the churches, and his influence was enormous.

In 1921, on the basis of his commentary *The Epistle to the Romans*, which he had published at the end of 1918, Barth was invited to Göttingen, to the newly established honorary chair of reformed theology. He totally revised that commentary for its second edition in 1922. Now his theological emphasis was more widely known and in print. In Göttingen he was in the thick of it. The professor of church history, appointed about the same time, was Emanuel Hirsch, a German Nationalist who worked for the reawakening of German pride and German strength. He later provided Hitler with all the ammunition he needed to show that the Protestant churches should support his anti-semitic policies.

Karl Barth's theology gave Christian pastors and lay people throughout Germany a way to use the Bible as a guide in the confusing times that followed defeat, cruel reparations, inflation and the rise of National Socialism. It was a theology for its time. Of course it was acceptable only to a minority, and mainly in the two thousand parishes of the Confessing Church. Barth left Göttingen for Bonn, and eventually had to retreat to Basel. But his influence remained. Under his influence the church purified and preserved itself. Even the Confessing Church would not risk its demise.

BONHOEFFER'S ACCEPTANCE AND REJECTION OF KARL BARTH

The influence of Karl Barth upon the young Dietrich Bonhoeffer is considerable. In 1924, at the age of eighteen, Bonhoeffer read Barth's *Theology and the Word of God*, which gave a new direction to his thinking. He championed Barth against Harnack in Berlin, and after a year in Union Theological Seminary, New York, he met him in Bonn in 1931.

Bonhoeffer remained a staunch supporter, but he was not uncritical. Their first quarrel was about his flight to London in 1933. Barth wanted him in the firing line, and saw the London pastorate as an escape. In many ways Bonhoeffer was more aware of the issues than Barth. When the Aryan Clause separated Jewish from Gentile Christians, Bonhoeffer reminded Barth of his statement that 'where a church adopted the Aryan clause it would cease to be a Christian Church'. He proposed breaking away from the state and becoming a Free Church. Barth advised caution and said to wait and see if things might get better. This was so often the attitude of the

churches – 'Wait! It may blow over. Meanwhile conform.'
The result was that resistance always came too late. Bonhoeffer saw this as the 'defensive attitude' of the church.
The church acted to preserve itself 'as an institute for salvation'. It was not prepared to take risks.

Bonhoeffer continued to ask for books by Barth to read
when he was in prison, and he was convinced that Barth had
started something he had to continue.

> If our final judgement must be that the western form of Christian-
> ity, too, was only a preliminary stage to a complete absence of
> religion, what kind of situation emerges for us, for the church?
> How can Christ become the Lord of the religionless as well? Are
> there religionless Christians? If religion is only a garment of
> Christianity – and even this garment has looked very different at
> different times – then what is a religionless Christianity?[8]

In that letter of 30 April 1944, Bonhoeffer recognises that he
is following Karl Barth, and does not think that Barth took it
far enough. 'Barth,' he continues, 'who is the only one to have
started along this line of thought, did not carry it to com-
pletion, but arrived at a positivism of revelation, which in the
last analysis is essentially a restoration.'[9] Bonhoeffer is convinced that this has nothing to say to a religionless generation.
The real question is not being faced. It is the relevance of a
church – sermons, liturgy, Christian way of life, community –
what relevance is it all to people without religion? How do we
speak about God without religion? How do we speak about
God in a secular way, or is it no longer possible to speak of
God?

Bonhoeffer was prepared to accept that he and those who
believed as he did were religionless and secular, like the great
majority of their contemporaries. Like Karl Barth, he saw
that Christ was no longer the object of religion. But he was
stepping into new territory when he asked about the church,
or the *Ekklesia*. The word means 'called forth', which, like
Barth, he would not interpret to mean specially favoured
from a religious point of view. Bonhoeffer insisted that the
church must belong wholly to the world. He emphasised the
common humanity of believer and non-believer alike. But his

unanswered question was, 'If Christ is no longer the object of religion (*i.e.* belonging in some special way to the church), what is he?' Something quite different: really the Lord of the world? But what does that mean? And again, what place does worship and prayer have in a religionless situation? He asked if the 'arcane discipline' has a special place here. In his letter to Bethge, he referred to the difference between the ultimate and the penultimate in this connection. For a fuller understanding of that we must go to his *Ethics*.[10] It is part of Bonhoeffer's movement away from Karl Barth, but we shall leave it for the moment.

What is more to the point immediately is that after an interruption, Bonhoeffer comes back with a quite new idea. As Barth had found enlightenment in Paul, both in his *The Epistle to the Romans* and in his awareness that he saw something that others did not see, so Bonhoeffer recalls what Paul said and did in his fight for the liberation of his young churches from circumcision. As Paul had asked if circumcision is a condition of justification, and had answered no, it must now be asked if religion is necessary to salvation. And then he adds:

> I often ask myself why a 'Christian instinct' often draws me more to the religionless people than to the religious, by which I don't in the least mean with any evangelizing intention, but, I might almost say, 'in brotherhood'. While I'm often reluctant to mention God by name to religious people – because that name somehow seems to me here not to ring true, and I feel myself to be slightly dishonest . . . – to people with no religion I can on occasion mention him by name quite calmly . . . Religious people speak of God when human knowledge . . . has come to an end, or when human resources fail.[11]

This is Bonhoeffer's theme pushed further. Religion brings in God at the boundaries of human knowledge and strength, exploiting human weakness. It can only be a temporary expedient until people can by their own strength push these boundaries further out. But such expedients are unworthy. Should we talk of human boundaries at all? 'Is even death, which people now hardly fear, and is sin, which they now hardly understand, still a genuine boundary today?'[12] The anxiety to reserve a space for God is making him too small. We must speak of God not at the boundaries of human experience but at the centre.

A week later, on 5 May 1944, Barth is getting a very rough ride. Admitting that Barth was the first theologian to begin the criticism of religion, Bonhoeffer complains that he put in its place a positive doctrine of revelation which says, in effect: '"Like it or lump it": Virgin birth, Trinity, or anything else; each is an equally significant and necessary part of the whole, which must simply be swallowed as a whole or not at all. That isn't biblical.'[13] Bonhoeffer insists on degrees of knowledge and degrees of significance. Barth's positivism of revelation sets up a law of faith. These things you are required to believe. How much do you have to swallow to be a Christian? This mutilates what by Christ's incarnation is a gift to us. In the place of religion, there now stands the church, while the world has to get on the best way it can. A church separated from the world is a mistake. A world separated from the church, left to its own devices, made to depend on itself, is also a mistake. Church and world must be in this religionless situation together. But how are we to understand in a worldly sense the great statement of the incarnation: 'And the Word became flesh and dwelt among us, full of grace and truth; we have beheld his glory, glory as of the only Son from the Father' (John 1:14)? And how, in that same sense, and with the background of the Old Testament, against which Bonhoeffer insists we must always read the New Testament, can we give a secular meaning to concepts like repentance, faith, forgiveness, rebirth?

There is a letter from Eberhard Bethge to Bonhoeffer on 3 June 1944 which raises the question many theologians of the Confessing Church must have been asking. Bethge had been discussing Bultmann with F. Justus Perels, the legal adviser to the Confessing Church, who thought that the Bultmann affair was settled: Rudolf Bultmann had gone too far, and must be 'excommunicated'. Bethge is surprised that the problem does not trouble Perels. He is worried about the general impression, even in the Confessing Church, that people want to have fixed concepts – despite everything. The Barth–

Bultmann–Bonhoeffer line has made tremendous progress in contrast to the liberal period. What is it that attracts people to Barth and the Confessing Church? Are they expecting a hoard of truth there? Is it the old attraction of the Old Testament prophets? Is it support for the oppressed? No one seems to be discussing these things, and in fact discussion is discouraged by the leap back into dogma. Bethge persists, nonetheless, and asks if Protestants are to 'lose ground' from one generation to the next:

> So, what are we to do about making particular claims on 'ground' in the world? What is the role of the cult and the prophet? Finally, what is the significance of the Christian tradition in which we stand? Of the 'conceptions' of people with which they are to be nourished and in which they have been nourished?[14]

Eberhard Bethge expresses his eagerness to hear Bonhoeffer's comments on Bultmann. He did not have long to wait. In a letter of 8 June 1944, Bonhoeffer returns to the theme of Barth's limitations. His great service remains: 'He brought in against religion the God of Jesus Christ, "*pneuma* against *sarx*".' But he gave no guidelines for the non-religious interpretation of theological concepts. That was his limitation, and because of it his theology of revelation became what Bonhoeffer calls a 'positivism of revelation'.[15]

Bonhoeffer further complains that the Confessing Church has forgotten all about the Barthian approach and has lapsed from positivism into conservative restoration. It seems to be exhausting itself in the effort to protect the great concepts of Christian theology. It has become a church on the defensive. Bonhoeffer is greatly disappointed, and in that mood turns to Bultmann, who seems to have recognised Barth's limitations. But he has misunderstood them and tried to correct the situation along liberal lines, following the typical liberal process of reduction: 'the "mythological" elements of Christianity are dropped, and Christianity is reduced to its "essence"'.[16] Bonhoeffer's comments on Bultmann are in this critical and slightly depressed mood. He is not seriously tackling the full meaning of Bultmann's *entmythologisierung*, but his comments are important. His own view is that the full content, including the 'mythological' concepts, must be kept – the New Testament is not a mythological clothing of a universal truth; this mythology (resurrection etc.) is the thing itself – but the concepts must be interpreted in such a way as not to make religion a precondition of faith . . . Only in that way, I think, will liberal theology be overcome . . . and at the same time its question be genuinely taken up and answered . . . Thus the world's coming of age is no longer an occasion for polemics and apologetics, but is now really better understood than it understands itself, namely on the basis of the gospel and in the light of Christ.[17]

With that letter Bonhoeffer has gone beyond Barth and questioned Bultmann's basic thesis. But he had neither peace nor strength to continue this exposition of his attempts to be of 'help for the church's future'.

'STATIONS ON THE ROAD TO FREEDOM'

After trying other ways of expressing his new thoughts for the future structure of the church and ways of understanding a religionless world which had come of age, Bonhoeffer turned to poetry. One of his best poems, 'Stations on the Road to Freedom',[18] has been studied as his own personal pilgrimage and as a description of an individual's road to freedom. It has rarely been seen as the liberation of the church from its defensive structures. Yet, here it has its most powerful message; and it comes at a time when the church is divided and controlled, imprisoned by its own structures and desperately in need of freedom.

After the defeat of Germany in May 1945, the churches of Germany had to be set free for their most important task of bringing life to a dead nation. This was particularly true because of the massacre of Germany's leadership following the failure of the plot to assassinate Hitler. At the end of the war, every perceptive visitor reported the divisions within the Protestant churches of Germany.

Those who had followed the courageous history of the Confessing Church against the German Christians (who would have handed the church over to Hitler as a compliant instrument), expected that after Germany's defeat the Confessing Church would have taken over the leadership. But they were not ready. Stewart Herman, visiting Martin Niemöller on 31 July 1945, reports:

> Niemöller seemed particularly exercised at finding the so-called 'neutral' church better organized to take charge of German church government than the Confessing Church, which according to him had done virtually nothing in the three months since the Nazi defeat . . . As a consequence, he felt that the 'neutrals' were getting back to work as though nothing had happened. He felt that the German Christians with their leadership principle had all the advantages over the Evangelical Church; whereas the Catholic Church stood to profit from a restoration of its 1925 status.[19]

This was what Bonhoeffer had feared. All was to return to normal. Instead of facing the new world with a religionless Christianity, the churches reverted to their past structures (including the restoration of the church tax).

Bonhoeffer's 'Stations on the Road to Freedom' assumes an immediate relevance when applied to the restrictive structures of the churches.[20]

Self-discipline
If you set out to seek freedom, you must learn before all
 things
Mastery over sense and soul, lest your wayward desirings,
Lest your undisciplined members lead you now this way,
 now that way.
Chaste be your mind and your body, and subject to you
 and obedient,
Serving solely to seek their appointed goal and objective.
None learns the secret of freedom save only by way of
 control.

Action
Do and dare what is right, not swayed by the whim of the
 moment.

Bravely take hold of the real, not dallying now with what
might be.
Not in the flight of ideas but only in action is freedom.
Make up your mind and come out into the tempest of
living.
God's command is enough and your faith in Him to
sustain you.
Then at last freedom will welcome your spirit amid great
rejoicing.

Suffering

See what a transformation! These hands so active and
powerful
Now are tied, and alone and fainting, you see where your
work ends.
Yet you are confident still, and gladly commit what is
rightful
Into a stronger hand, and say that you are contented.
You were free for a moment of bliss, then you yielded
your freedom
Into the hand of God, that He might perfect it in glory.

Death

Come now, highest of feasts on the way to freedom
eternal,
Death, strike off the fetters, break down the walls that
oppress us,
Our bedazzled soul and our ephemeral body,
That we may see at last the sight which here was not
vouchsafed us.
Freedom, we sought you long in discipline, action,
suffering.
Now as we die we see you and know you at last, face to
face.

1 Discipline (Zucht)

The image is that of the body, which is a familiar New
Testament image for the church. The beginning of the search

for freedom is to discipline the senses (*Sinne*) and the soul or self (*Seele*), so that the longings and the members (*Begierde* and *Gliede*) do not pull you this way and that.

Of course this fits the chaos of sexual desires, but it is banal if it applies only to that. The sexual turmoil of a young man in times of temptation is adequately matched by the confusion of the Protestant churches in Hitler's Germany and after.

The key word comes in the next line – 'Chaste' (*Keusch*) be your spirit and your body, completely under your own control and obedient. Obedient to what and to whom?: 'to seek the goal set it'. The need for the liberated church to begin with discipline and obedience to its proper goal is evident. The goal is that set by God for the church as well as the individual for society.

'Chaste' is a word associated with 'pure' (*züchtig*). This is not a call for monastic celibacy, but rather an echo of two New Testament phrases, James' 'unspotted by the world' and Paul's 'stripped for action', which is the next station. The first station is summed up as, 'No one experiences the secret of freedom, except through discipline.'

In the post-war world, it has become even more evident that the independence of 'discipline' of this kind was the first charge laid upon the churches of the world. A church which is on the defensive is not disciplined, but pulled this way and that; while an undisciplined church dare not take risks. When the Church of England looked at the Urban Priority Areas and admitted its failures, as well as those of the government, its report *Faith in the City* was not defensive and it most certainly took risks. This was immediately evident when the government attacked it. The Lambeth Conference of 1988 has shown similar discipline in holding the Anglican Communion together, while it tackled honestly and with courage the issues of the ordination of women, the open attitude to sexual mores such as polygamy and homosexuality, and the problem of violence in South Africa. It may only be the first station, but it is the first requirement, for 'No one experiences the secret of freedom, except through discipline.'

2 Action (Tat)

This is Faust's terminus in Goethe's drama, as he grows
increasingly dissatisfied with the translation of *logos* in the
Prologue to the Fourth Gospel. What is the root of it all – 'In
the beginning was the *Word*' – seems inadequate, as indeed it
is, and he tries 'Thought', 'Power', and finally '*die Tat*' (the
deed or action). The poodle interrupts his work, but he has
already indicated some satisfaction with the word '*Tat*', for he
writes, 'The spirit comes to guide me in my need, I write, "In
the beginning was the Deed".'

We cannot for ever weigh the pros and cons. Bonhoeffer
spoke from terrible experience. All are aware of the debilitat-
ing effect of indecision. The choice is between 'what you *like*'
and 'what is *right*'. Once that is dimly discerned, the venture
must be made in action. The besetting sin of all institutions,
including churches, is to postpone until they are sure and safe.
The South African churches have had to face the truth of that,
and it is significant that Alan Boesak, one of the leading
and most courageous church leaders at this period in South
Africa, is a Bonhoeffer scholar. Speaking in Amsterdam at
the 1988 Bonhoeffer Congress, he attributed his attitude to
apartheid to the influence of Bonhoeffer. The decisive step to
outlaw racism from the church as a heresy, he said, was
comparable with the reaction of the Confessing Church in
Germany to the German Christians. In 1934, the Barmen
Declaration was accepted as a Confession; in South Africa,
apartheid created a situation in which a new Confession was
needed. One was drafted by the churches of the South
African Council of Churches. Racism was named as a heresy
in this new Confession. But as the Confessing Church stopped
short of including a reference to anti-semitism, so the South
African Churches have hesitated to speak clearly about the
use of violence. Sooner or later, as Alan Boesak and Desmond Tutu have frequently pointed out, the situation may
require the churches to support violence. That would be to
risk world condemnation. The relevance of this second
station becomes evident.

'Not weighing the possibilities, but bravely grasping *the*

real.' 'The real' (*das Wirkliche*) means that the church must act upon the reality of the situation and not upon theoretical principles. 'Freedom is not to be found in discussion, but only in *action.*'

And then Bonhoeffer appeals, and his appeal is needed still: 'Come away from your anxious hesitations, into the storm, where the action is.' But who can you trust, and might you not be wrong? That has to be risked, but there is some guidance, and it is all the church has: 'God's command . . . and your faith.'

When the church can face the real situation, listen to God and have faith, it will not set up a commission to discuss what should be done, it will act. What lies behind that courageous act, which has not counted the cost, is a disciplined study of God's word, a knowledge of God's command which grows out of obedience, and a total faith in God's rule. Then the church is free. 'Freedom will welcome your spirit with joy.'

3 Suffering

The suffering servant of Second Isaiah is the personification of a people. It is God's way with those he loves, his chosen people. They never like it, but learn to discover it as the only way. In Isaiah 49 this is most clearly set out. The servant complains that he has been given all the promises, that he has been prepared for victory, that he has been told that through him God will display his splendour (vv. 1–3). But there are no victories and little evidence of splendour; the servant people are defeated refugees in a foreign land (v. 4). God admits all this, but his own statement is that the suffering servant has been too concerned with his own preservation, much as Bonhoeffer complained in his day that his church 'had been fighting only for its own preservation'. God shows to Israel a greater glory that comes, not by might or power, but by the mysterious ways of his Spirit:

It is too small a thing for you to be my servant
  to restore the tribes of Jacob
  and bring back those of Israel I have kept.

> I will also make you a light for the Gentiles,
>> that you may bring my salvation to the ends of the
>>> earth.

(Isaiah 49:6, NIV)

No triumphalism for Israel and no triumphalism for the church of Christ. The disciplined and obedient church must learn to accept failure and, what is even more difficult to accept, replacement by others.

If this third station applies only to the individual or to Bonhoeffer's own experience, it is moving, good advice to someone too long in office, a hint at Bonhoeffer's acceptance that he will not live to take part in the rebuilding of his nation and church when the war is over. But there is surely more here than that. This is the crucial sacrifice of the church itself, accepting the 'wonderful change'. Its hands are bound now. Once it followed the road to freedom by discipline and action, bravely stepping out into the storm where the action is. And it was cut down.

The phenomenal decline of the churches in Europe has been read only as failure; the wealthy and growing congregations, first of America and then of Africa and parts of Asia, the charismatic growth and attraction, have all been read as success. It is possible that an aged Christian, seeing the success of the charismatic movement and the decline of the traditional churches he has served all his life, may read this third station with consolation:

> A change has come indeed. Your hands so strong and active,
> are bound; in helplessness now you see your action
> is ended; you sigh in relief, your cause committing
> to stronger hands; so now you may rest contented.

But there is surely more here than the consolation of an aged Christian who is no longer able to be active. The letters that Bonhoeffer was writing about this time were not about resignation, but about change.

What if these lines refer to the churches – that is the church as we know it: bound, helpless, its action ended? Can the church which has lived with all the honours of two thousand

years 'sigh in relief' to give it all up? Having drawn so near to
touch freedom, 'can it give it back to God', trusting him to
perfect that freedom in glory? If this crucial station is applied
to the church as an institution, it means being prepared to give
everything back to God, in order to be free. This is a real risk.
Perhaps a slightly more literal translation will bring out the
revolutionary nature of this stanza:

> Wonderful transformation. The strong and active hands
>   are bound.
> Powerless and alone, you see the end of your action.
> Yet, you breathe a sigh of relief and, laying aside the right
> that you had chosen to act upon, you trusted it to a hand
> stronger than yours and were contented.
> Freedom blessed you only for a moment, then you gave it
>   back to
> God, in order that he might perfect it in glory.

A disciplined people who had been prepared to act upon what
they saw to be right and risked the opposition that came from
within and without, tasting for a moment the freedom of not
compromising and doing what they were sure had to be done,
are defeated and see no future for the institution they loved.
Now what will they do? Fight for their own preservation? Or,
the most risky throw of all, trust God? Even if God is to do it
without them?

4   Death

Can the church allow God to choose another way? That step
leads to the fourth station, which on this interpretation is the
death of the church. Perhaps the history of the church, as we
know it, is limited, and it must learn how to die.

One is reminded of Karl Barth's address at Tambach:

> *The Christian*: we must be agreed that we do not mean *the
> Christians*, not the multitude of the baptized, nor the chosen few
> who are Religious Socialists, nor even the cream of the noblest
> and most devoted Christians we might think of. The Christian is
> *the Christ*.[21]

But as usual, Barth did not follow it through. More to the point, perhaps, are Bonhoeffer's own words in the Baptism sermon:

> Our church, which has been fighting in these years only for its self-preservation, as though that were an end in itself, is incapable of taking the word of reconciliation and redemption to mankind and the world. Our earlier words are therefore bound to lose their force and cease, and our being Christians today will be limited to two things: prayer and righteous action among men. All Christian thinking, speaking, and organizing must be born anew out of this prayer and action. By the time you have grown up, the church's form will have changed greatly. We are not yet out of the melting-pot, and any attempt to help the church prematurely to a new expansion of its organization will merely delay its conversion and purification. It is not for us to prophesy the day (though the day will come) when men will once more be called so to utter the word of God that the world will be changed and renewed by it. It will be a new language, perhaps quite non-religious, but liberating and redeeming – as was Jesus' language; it will shock people and yet overcome them by its power; it will be the language of a new righteousness and truth, proclaiming God's peace with men and the coming of his kingdom.[22]

In the light of that passage, which occasionally rises to John's vision of a New Jerusalem (Revelation 21 and 22), we can read the last stanza with the church in mind, as well as the individual – dying to live:

> Come now, highest feast on the way to eternal freedom,
> death, destroy the heavy chains and restricting walls
> of our temporal bodies and blinded souls,
> that we may at last catch a glimpse of what is here
>   begrudged us.
> Freedom, we sought you long in discipline, action,
>   suffering.
> Dying we recognize you now, in the face of God himself.[23]

Part 2

The Real Meaning of Christian Faith

INTRODUCTION

The year 1956 was one of those decisive moments in history which Stefan Zweig called *Sternstunden*, no doubt meaning originally, 'the hour which the stars had decreed'. The armed forces of the Warsaw Pact invaded Hungary and put an end to the dream of world communism as a unity; Britain made her last imperial gesture when with France and Israel she invaded Egypt.

So many big and little things happened in that year at the height of the Cold War that it is impossible not to see its lasting significance. It prepared the way for the student revolts of the 1960s. In popular theology it prepared the way for John Robinson's *Honest to God*. If that broke upon a startled Christian community, it was only because the radical thinking that lay at the heart of it had been until then confined to academics and theologians. Ideas were not yet in motion, but they were there, and so dangerous for the stability of the existing order that they were, on the whole, hushed up. I recall a television programme in the 1960s discussing the content of John Robinson's controversial paperback, when Daniel Jenkins was asked if he was surprised by some of the ideas the Bishop had proclaimed. He said, 'No. I might have been if I had not been living with them already for years.'

It is in this setting that John Bowden opens his book *Jesus: The Unanswered Questions* with an account of an experience in an Oxford college chapel in 1956. There he heard from his tutor Christopher Evans, for the first time, words which, as he says, have haunted him ever since. They were Bonhoeffer's words from prison: 'What is bothering me incessantly is the question what Christianity really is, or indeed who Christ really is, for us today.'[1]

That question has haunted a generation. It is not a new one. Ever since the critical work of Wellhausen on the Old Testament led him to resign his post at Greifswald, because he thought that his critical teaching was making his students unsuitable for ministry, biblical criticism has questioned the accepted answer. And that was in the 1880s! Biblical scholars have not generally set out with the intention of destroying a simple faith in the Bible, but there is no doubt that biblical criticism has made it impossible to read the Bible without questioning it.

John Bowden's book is a radical examination of many of the cherished doctrines of simple Christians, and indeed also of very sophisticated ones who fight a rearguard action against change. In his Preface, he gives his reasons for all this questioning. One is a passionate concern for truth, but the most persuasive reason is the first, a personal one, which he shares with many, including Bonhoeffer:

> For all its questioning, this book is written out of a deep and positive faith in God, to whom I cannot say no, a faith which I have to acknowledge originated through the Jesus about whom I ask so many questions. I have to ask the questions, because they are there to be asked, and if God is, then God is to be found, or to find me, through these questions and not by avoiding them. Jesus is extremely question-able, but nevertheless he is somehow worth bothering about because by asking all the questions one comes up against the reality of how things still are. At least many people do.[2]

That is 'authentic theology', and Bonhoeffer would have warmed to it.

5

GOD AND WORLDLINESS

When Carl Gustav Jung, the psychologist of the unconscious, was asked, 'Do you believe in God?', he replied, 'I don't believe, I know.' That is a laudable confession of certainty, but it confuses the meaning of faith. Faith is not a faltering search in the dark recesses of life, but the confidence we have in all we hope for; it is the guarantee of all that we know to be important, but it is not accessible to logical investigation alone. The most obvious parallel is human love, which is only possible on the basis of trust. Two people are attracted to each other, and there are basic biological reasons for this, but no true lovers are satisfied with purely biological or chemical explanations. Their love has first of all a social setting, the context of meeting. It grows through common interests, and there are meetings of minds which are built upon the biological foundations. But there is also a transcendence in human love. Biology and chemistry do not produce poetry and the urge to write poetry or to discover the poetry of others, uncovering new thoughts and feelings, is almost universal. Common interests and a sense of transcendence do not dissolve the biological attraction, but they transform and even intensify it. At every stage of development there is a need for trust, for faith in the partner. For what no lover can tolerate is the denial of uniqueness in his or her relationship. That is the more worthy basis of jealousy, which is not always fully explained as possessiveness: it can be a fear that the relationship is not unique. The transcendence of love is so near to what traditionally we describe as religious transcendence, *i.e.* the transcendent quality of God and his activities, that religion is often brought into the relationship of human love. There is, however, a danger here which Bonhoeffer pointed out in his sermon[1] to Eberhard and Renate Bethge on their wedding day:

> It is right and proper for a bride and bridegroom to welcome and celebrate their wedding day with a unique sense of triumph . . . The children of the earth are rightly proud of being allowed to take a hand in shaping their own destinies, and something of this pride must contribute to the happiness of a bride and bridegroom. We ought not to be in too much of a hurry here to speak piously of God's will and guidance. It is obvious, and it should not be ignored, that it is your own very human wills that are at work here, celebrating their triumph; the course that you are taking at the outset is one that you have chosen for yourselves; what you have done and are doing is not, in the first place, something religious, but something quite secular. So you yourselves, and you alone, bear the responsibility for what no one can take from you; or, to put it more exactly, you, Eberhard, have all the responsibility for the success of your venture, with all the happiness that such responsibility involves . . .[2]

Bonhoeffer continues in a way that would hardly please the feminists, but he was writing in 1943, and within a masculine culture. Renate would not today be satisfied with merely helping her husband to bear that responsibility, as Bonhoeffer says! But leaving that lapse to one side, he continues, assuming joint responsibilities: 'Unless you can boldly say today: "That is *our* resolve, *our* love, *our* way", you are taking refuge in a false piety.'[3]

But Bonhoeffer does insist that God adds his 'Yes' to their 'Yes' and guides their marriage, making it indissoluble, establishing a rule of life within marriage, laying both a blessing and a burden upon them. These things cause both man and wife to call upon God, and should remind them of their eternal destiny in his kingdom. This allows them to see their marriage as more than the union of two people and the building of a family.

'Earthly society', he adds, 'is only the beginning of the heavenly society, the earthly home an image of the heavenly home, the earthly family a symbol of the fatherhood of God over all men, for they are his children.'[4] Here God and the world are related to each other in a dynamic way, not in two separate compartments. If it is true that everything we can responsibly know or say about God goes to the heart of this life and its responsibilities, then in this sermon Bonhoeffer shows the dynamic response. Everything which calls forth a response in this life is related to our experience of God. In that sense, Bonhoeffer says to the married couple: 'God gives you Christ as the foundation of your marriage'; but not until he has made it clear that it was no religious act they entered into when they accepted responsibility for what they are doing. The gift of Christ as the foundation of the marriage now means that they can live together in the forgiveness of their sins, 'for without it no human fellowship, least of all a marriage, can survive'.[5]

Bonhoeffer in this sermon and in the subsequent letters makes it quite clear that he does not relinquish eschatology and transcendence, but as Bethge comments:

> He did not dream of identifying God and the world. On the contrary, he wanted to rediscover genuine transcendence by drawing it down from its aloofness. God and the world are not one and the same thing, but God and worldliness belong together as truly as God is God.[6]

As in many other cases, we have got to go to Bonhoeffer's *Ethics* in order to clarify and extend that thought. There we find him recovering the real concept of the secular, which he defends against the attacks of pietism. His concept of the secular sees it as 'the movement of being accepted and becoming accepted by God in Christ'.[7] This is part of Bonhoeffer's refusal to think in terms of two spheres, or pairs of mutually exclusive terms like 'secular' and 'Christian', 'natural' and 'supernatural', 'sacred' and 'profane', or 'rational' and 'revelational'.

The Unity of 'Opposites' in the Reality of Christ

There is a need to break away from the old concept of two armed camps. In the one is the church, trafficking in the

supernatural, the sacred and revelation. In the other camp is
the secular world (what else can the world be but secular?),
living by natural reason, within the limits of a profane existence. The one is good, the other evil. Such thinking gives rise
to such lines in our hymnbooks as

> Glorious things of thee are spoken,
> Zion, city of our God!
> He whose word cannot be broken
> Formed thee for his own abode:
> On the Rock of Ages founded,
> What can shake thy sure repose?
> With salvation's walls surrounded,
> Thou may'st smile at all thy foes.[8]

The church is seen as an impregnable fortress, where God
dwells ('. . . his own abode'). The abuses of the world outside
are no concern of the happy and secure dwellers within, who
'smile at all *their foes*'. Neither is it simply poetic licence. The
figure is maintained in our attitude to evangelism, as skirmishes to capture a few of the world and bring them into the
protection of 'salvation's walls'.

How much more robust are the words of the gospels. In the
scene described on the mount of transfiguration, Peter wants
to erect three tents for Moses, Elijah and Christ. There he
would stay: 'It is good for us to be here.' The response to his
proposal is that he should pay attention to God's 'beloved
Son'. And that Son takes them down from their vision,
imposing a vow of silence, and into a world where a father is in
despair because the disciples have failed to heal his son
(Matthew 17:1–21). The gospels recognise such holy places
and moments, but they are transitory. From these places, the
witnesses go out for the sake of the world. In the Fourth
Gospel, they are told that they are 'in the world', even if their
vision of the Christ has made them no longer 'conformed to
the world' (John 17:11–19). This is a more dynamic form of
evangelism: people are not rescued out of the world, but
redeemed in the world and there they remain.

The classic passage in Matthew 16:13–20, which tells of
Jesus building his church on the foundation of Peter's faith

and vision, does not speak of a space for the church. It is founded on the rock of a very human disciple (and that means all disciples and witnesses), and it has no walls. Its strength lies not in its defences, but in the knowledge that Jesus is 'the Christ, the Son of the living God'. The power (or 'ages') of the evil one will not overcome it. The conflict between good and evil is in the world. Even the keys of the kingdom are given on earth, in the world, to be used on earth, even if they have currency in heaven. The disciples are seen as 'salt', preserving the world from corruption, or as a light shining in the darkness of despair (Matthew 5:13–14).

Of course, there is a space where religious acts are performed. There the witnesses assemble, there prayer is poured out, the bread is broken, the apostolic teaching is heard (Acts 2:43–47). But that space is part of the world, and is no more holy than any other space. It is like the room where the disciple goes to pray, having carefully shut the door that he may 'pray to his Father in secret' (Matthew 6:6). But it can be any room, and such a room can be used for other so-called 'secular' purposes.

With consummate skill the author of the Epistle to the Hebrews dismantles the temple and dispenses with the holy priests. Now Christ has replaced them all. The temple we enter is no separated holy place, but through his body we enter into the presence of God our Father:

> Therefore, brothers, since we have confidence to enter the Most Holy Place by the blood of Jesus, by a new and living way opened for us through the curtain, that is, his body, and since we have a great high priest over the house of God, let us draw near to God with a sincere heart in full assurance of faith . . . (Hebrews 10:19–22, NIV)

The new covenant has made all the requirements of the old redundant. Now we have direct access to God. There is still the need to assemble together, to encourage one another in good works (Hebrews 10:25); but this is not a segregated piece of the world. We are 'in the world'. And we continue under the knowledge that 'God so loved *the world* that he gave his only Son'. His intention is that all the world should be

saved, that 'whoever believes in him should not perish but
have eternal life' (John 3:16). And as the statement continues, 'God sent the Son into the world, not to condemn the
world, but that *the world might be saved through him*' (John
3:17).

The New Testament concept of the church as the 'body of
Christ' is therefore not intended primarily as representing the
separation of the church from the world. The gospel insistence upon a full incarnation of Christ makes the vision of the
body of Christ an image of all people taken up and enclosed
within the body. The believers have seen this vision and bear
witness to its truth. When Jesus says that his disciples are to be
his witnesses, this is what they bear witness to – that humanity
is taken up in the body of Christ. They must do this by their
words and their lives. Rather than thinking of the church as so
pure that it must not be soiled by contact with the world, the
world is summoned into the fellowship of this body of Christ,
to which in truth it really belongs. There is a distinction
between the church and the world, just as there is a clear
distinction between the world and God. But as God is related
to the world by his creating and sustaining power, so the
church is related to the world by its affirmation of God's
acceptance of humanity. The world does not affirm this, and
therefore the church witnesses to its reality by allowing it to
take effect in the church.

> The body of Jesus Christ, especially as it appears to us on the
> cross, shows to the eyes of faith the world in its sin, and how it is
> loved by God, no less than it shows the Church, as the congrega-
> tion of those who acknowledge their sin and submit to the love of
> God.[9]

The church and the world are, of course, different from each
other. But this difference must not be expressed in terms of
impregnable walls or fixed border lines. They are not two
hostile camps. The church must bear witness to the truth that
God and the world are 'at one' in Christ.

CHRIST AND THE WORLD

The New Testament says quite dogmatically, and many times, that the world was made by Christ and 'without him was not anything made that was made' (John 1:3). The world is created through him, and he is its omega point, or goal. It therefore consists in Christ. I mean the world, not the church only, but the church as part of the world also. But how to distinguish without separation?

Bonhoeffer talks of the world being 'relative to Christ', whether it knows it or not.[10] This relativeness is made concrete in what he calls 'mandates'. This word is used instead of 'orders of creation', because he means that they are imposed by God, and are not the essential nature of humanity. He finds four such mandates in the scriptures: labour, marriage, government and the church.[11]

In these mandates the relation of Christ to the world assumes concrete forms. The church is only one of them, however important. But it is different from the first three. We can find the first three in the Old Testament – in the Garden of Eden and the union of Adam and Eve after the Fall, and the respect for these first two mandates in the third, in government. The divine mandate of the church, however, is the task of enabling the reality of Jesus Christ to be manifest in its preaching, organisation and way of life. It is concerned with the external salvation of the world, of which it is part. This does not mean that it conquers the world. There is no place for triumphalism in the church. It bears witness, and all humanity is involved. The triumph of the church is in dissolving the barriers which the world rather than the church has erected. Thus the mandate of the church impinges upon the other three mandates, because now we see that the Christian also is the labourer, the partner in marriage and the subject of government. The three mandates are intended to unify the person, not divide. This is the whole person in the world and before God, as Creator, Reconciler, and Redeemer. And they are supremely witnessed to in the Christian.

All four mandates are one in the incarnate God, Jesus Christ. In this he represents all humanity. He represents women as well as men. In this earthly life he did not marry. He represented male and female in the marriage partnership. So we see that in his dealings with men and women he is able to relate to either as the partner. There are few details of his labour, but he represented the labour of all who came in contact with him, from a fisherman to a tax-collector. He was subject to the government – paying taxes to Caesar, and yet knowing what belonged to God. By example and by the guidance of his disciples he represented the first three mandates. Of the fourth he was the author – building his church in the earthiness of Peter's confession, with a foundation no surer than the wavering loyalty of a human. Yet, it had to be. A fallible church, making real the presence of Jesus Christ, in whom God reconciled the world unto himself.

THE NON-RELIGIOUS INTERPRETATION OF BIBLICAL CONCEPTS

> . . . so to utter the word of God that the world will be changed and renewed by it. It will be a new language perhaps quite non-religious, but liberating and redeeming – as was Jesus' language; it will shock people and yet overcome them by its power; it will be the language of a new righteousness and truth, proclaiming God's peace with men and the coming of his kingdom.[12]

That was Bonhoeffer's vision, and he was sure that the day would come when it was realised. And are we ready for such a day? Inevitably a religion develops a private language because it has to express experiences not shared outside the community. But if Bonhoeffer was right in seeing the church as a witnessing community which is part of the world and not separate from it, then it has a communication problem. There is no place for a private language, however cherished. When we turn to the Greek New Testament, we find many of the religious terms did not begin as private symbols, but became such and in hallowed translation this was exaggerated. The development of modern translations since Bonhoeffer's death has been resisted by those who cherished the private

experience, but has been welcomed by those who recognised
the church's problems with communicating to a new generation. In England, the first of the new translations to emerge
from the wartime experience with young people was J. B.
Phillips' *Letters to Young Churches*.[13]

In 1941 Phillips saw the difficulty that young people had in
responding to the language of the Bible. He recognised the
relevance of Paul to the precarious situation of a Christian in
wartime Britain and translated the Epistle to the Colossians
for his youth club. A comparison between Colossians 1:15–20
in the venerable Authorised Version and in this new translation will show how Phillips went part of the way to giving
biblical terms a non-religious form. He took one step away
from the private language:

PHILLIPS	AV
Now Christ is the *visible expression* of the invisible God. He was born before creation began, for it was through him that everything was made, whether heavenly or earthly, seen or unseen. Through him, and for him, also, were created *power* and dominion, *ownership* and *authority*. In fact, all things were created through and for him. He is both the *first principle* and the *upholding principle* of the whole scheme of creation. And now he is the Head of the Body which is the Church. He is the beginning, the first to be born from the dead, which gives him pre-eminence over all things. It was in him that *the*	[Christ] is the *image* of the invisible God, the firstborn of every creature. For by him were all things created, that are in heaven, and that are in earth, visible and invisible, whether they be *thrones*, or dominions, or *principalities*, or *powers*. All things were created by him, and for him. And he is *before all things*, and *by him all things consist*. And he is the head of the body, the church: who is the beginning, the firstborn from the dead; that in all things he might have the preeminence. For it pleased the Father *that in him should all fulness dwell*; and, having made peace through the blood of his cross, by him *to*

full nature of God chose to live, and through him *God planned to reconcile* to his own person everything on earth and everything in Heaven, making peace by virtue of Christ's death on the cross.	*reconcile all things unto himself*; by him, I say, whether they be things in earth, or things in heaven.

Apart from his modernising of the language, Phillips' rendering is a very small step away from the mythology of religion. It is still religious language. I have put in italics those changes that represent the small step away: *visible expression* in place of *image*; *ownership* and *authority* instead of *thrones* and *principalities*, with *power* instead of *powers*; *first principle* and *upholding principle* instead of *before all things* and *by him all things consist*; *the full nature of God chose to live* instead of *it pleased the Father that in him should all fulness dwell*; and finally, *God planned to reconcile* instead of *by him to reconcile all things unto himself*. Although it makes much easier reading, this is not far removed from the AV, except that it has managed to struggle out of the medieval world.

In 1962, Kenneth Taylor produced a paraphrase of the passage in his *Living Letters*:[14]

> Christ is the exact likeness of the unseen God. He existed before God made anything at all, and, in fact, Christ himself is the Creator who made everything in heaven and earth, the things we can see and the things we can't; the spirit world with its kings and kingdoms, its rulers and authorities: all were made by Christ for his own use and glory. He was before all else began and it is his power that holds everything together. He is the Head of the body made up of his people – that is, his church – which he began; and he is the leader of all who arise from the dead, so that he is first in everything: for God wanted all of himself to be in his Son.

That is about as far as you can go with modern translations or paraphrases that explain the meaning of the passage. But the concepts are still religious. This is not really a new language, certainly not non-religious. In our present intellectual environment, can it be said to be liberating and redeeming? In

fact, is it like the language of Jesus? I think not. Something
more radical is needed, and it may be shocking, intending to
overcome those it shocks by its power. 'A new language',
then, 'of a new righteousness and truth, proclaiming God's
peace with men and the coming of his kingdom'. Bonhoeffer
said that it may have to be non-religious, because we speak to
people in a religionless world. But let us go as far as we can
with this passage from Colossians.

It says first of all that we can see God in the person of Jesus.
That means that if we present Jesus Christ in all his fullness –
human, weak, suffering humiliation, a preacher and a healer,
who triumphed over death itself – then we are presenting all
that humans can know of God. How important is it to present
a pre-existent Christ, who was the instrument of creation?
That perhaps tells us more about this man in whom we see
God. This is remote from our experience, but makes more
credible his claim to reveal all that we can know of God.

WHO IS JESUS CHRIST?

In other words, the question 'Who is Jesus Christ for us
today?' can only be answered if we have faced the prior
question: 'Who is Jesus Christ?'

It is surprising how few hard facts we have about him! *The
Quest of the Historical Jesus*, by Albert Schweitzer,[15] was a
classic survey of German Christology, but it ended with an
explanation which was heavily influenced by Schweitzer's
own Christology. *The Jesus of History*, by T. R. Glover,[16]
contained a good deal of excellent historical research, but the
public orator at Cambridge used his imagination and brilliant
style to reconstruct a lively picture of what he thought Jesus
was like. None of these – and there were many successors to
Schweitzer and Glover, continuing into the 1980s with TV
series such as *Jesus the Evidence* or *Jesus of Nazareth* and
controversial films – has done more to fill out the hard facts
with imaginative interpretations and background studies.

Only the most eccentric scholars doubt that Jesus lived in
Galilee roughly at the beginning of the period we mark as
Anno Domini. Dates of birth and death are uncertain. He was

baptised by John the Baptist, a prophet better known to
Jewish and Roman history than Jesus. Jesus was in the same
line as John, and probably appeared to succeed him. He
preached and healed the sick. He called disciples, and they
were spoken of as 'The Twelve', although many more followed him. He did not travel far outside his native land,
confining his activities to what today we would call Israel. He
was in repeated controversy with the Jewish religious authorities, particularly about the temple. He was crucified outside the walls of Jerusalem by the Roman authorities. After
his death his followers continued in a growing religious
movement which appeared to be a sect of Judaism, from
which it later broke away. There was continued hostility
between some Christians and some Jews who retained their
orthodox faith. By its very nature, there are few hard facts
about the resurrection of Jesus from the dead. His followers
believed that the tomb was empty on Easter morning, and
many of them testified to seeing him alive after his death.
None of these facts is likely to be changed by historical
research. Within a generation, his followers were convinced
that his resurrection was a guarantee of theirs. He had gone
before them and awaited their arrival at a place, or in a state
of consciousness, where they would be with him. On this
basis, they posed the question, as the disciples had in his
lifetime, 'Who is he?' The Jewish believers said, 'He is the
Messiah.' And very early, 'Christ' was added to 'Jesus' almost
like a second name – 'Jesus Christ' or 'Jesus Messiah'. But
coupled to this was 'Son of God', not in the Greek sense of
mythology, but in the Hebrew sense as inheriting all the
powers of God. This was consistent with the preaching of the
resurrection. It showed his power over life and death. But it
was not consistent with the crucifixion, which to Jewish
believers was a scandal, and to Gentile believers a stumbling-
block.

PAUL'S REINTERPRETATION

To many of the early Christians, Paul must have seemed a
little like John Robinson in the 1960s or David Jenkins in the

1980s. He was completely changing the way in which a generation had looked at Jesus. He appeared to have little interest in the life of Jesus or his vivid teaching in parables. There was only the occasional reference to the teaching of Jesus. Two things needed explaining, and Paul went straight to them in all his letters – the cross and the resurrection. Paul's teaching on the work of salvation wrought by Christ represents, broadly speaking, his attempt to reinterpret the primitive material which is preserved in the synoptic gospels along lines that would be meaningful to the urban, largely Gentile, communities with which he worked. Although his writing is still in religious terms, there is a reinterpretation which is similar to the task that Bonhoeffer required of us to discover 'a new language, perhaps quite non-religious, but liberating and redeeming'.

Paul gave to Christ a cosmic setting and set the stage for a world religion. His successors were the Fourth Gospel and the Epistle to the Hebrews.

Christ was before all time, the Son of God, who emptied himself 'of all but love' and came down into our experience. In the world, he showed all the nature of God that we could understand and taught people how to live and relate to each other. Ultimately, he was rejected and accepted the humiliation of the cross, where he came so low in human experience as to feel a separation from his Father. He was tempted like all human beings, and towards the end shrank from the cross. But it was his Father's will. He embraced the cross, and never was he nearer to his Father than at that moment when he died for the sins of the world. Then, in truth, 'God was in Christ, reconciling the world to himself' (2 Corinthians 5:19, NEB). After the resurrection, he prepared his followers to be his representatives, his ambassadors, so that the appeal of God might go on: '. . . and he has entrusted us with the message of reconciliation. We come therefore as Christ's ambassadors. It is as if God were appealing to you through us: in Christ's name, we implore you, be reconciled to God!' (Corinthians: 20, NEB).

This is more than a personal appeal, one to one, it is an appeal to all humanity, for 'Christ died for all'. The cosmic view is most evident in Romans 8. There Paul depicts the reconciliation of all created things to God, accomplished by the pioneers who have been transformed by Christ's death and been adopted as children of God – 'the creation itself will be set free from its bondage to decay and obtain the glorious liberty of the children of God' (Romans 8:21). This is an eschatology of hope. Christians live in the awareness of becoming children of God. This requires a lifestyle, but the lifestyle does not accomplish it. Christ has set that process in motion on the cross and in our acceptance of his claims, we believe and are in possession of 'the first fruits of the Spirit'. It is however a process, and we are impatient – 'groaning inwardly as we wait for adoption as sons, the redemption of our bodies' (Romans 8:23).

The worship of the church is in this way an expression of the groaning or eager waiting. The Lord's Supper, which is at the heart of worship, is described as a memorial service, 'in remembrance of me', but also an anticipation, 'as often as you eat this bread and drink the cup, you proclaim the Lord's death until he comes' (1 Corinthians 11: 25–26). The eager prayer of the church is '*Maranatha*' – 'Our Lord, come!' (1 Corinthians 16:22; *cf*. Revelation 22:20).

There is no doubt that, while it is foolish to say that Paul betrayed the faith of the early church and invented a new religion, it is certainly true that he reinterpreted the earliest material. But he was still writing in the first century, and within the framework of his religion. He was a Jew, and he was much influenced by the Greek thought of his day. If we are to fulfil Bonhoeffer's plans, we need to reinterpret Paul in terms of our thinking in a world dominated by scientific thought and largely without any sense of the presence of God. It is a world in which it is even dangerous to use the words 'God' or 'religion', because they have been so soiled and misused. When we speak of 'Christians' in the Lebanon or 'Catholics' in Ireland, we have debased the language and find it difficult to use. But Paul gives us one further help in his fight to break down the wall caused by circumcision. If religion has divided humanity so cruelly in our day, we may find, as Bonhoeffer does, a parallel in circumcision in Paul's day.

How then would the following passage in Galatians read if for 'circumcision' we read 'religion', or 'Catholic' or 'Protestant'!

Now I, Paul, say to you that if you receive *circumcision*, Christ will be of no advantage to you. I testify again to every man who receives *circumcision* that he is bound to keep the whole law. You are severed from Christ, you who would be justified by the law; you have fallen away from grace. For through the Spirit, by faith, we wait for the hope of righteousness. For in Christ Jesus neither *circumcision* nor *uncircumcision* is of any avail, but faith working through love. (Galatians 5:2–6).

If we follow Bonhoeffer's transposition of 'religion' for 'circumcision', we can read in that passage that 'religion' gives us no advantage. Once we are bound up with 'religion' (which means being bound) we have a burden upon us to keep the 'laws' (for religion is binding of laws). Such an attitude cuts us off from Christ. We try to 'be religious' and thus fall away from grace. It is only through the Spirit that we receive the hope of righteousness. Religious or irreligious is irrelevant. Faith works through love.

What follows in Bonhoeffer's summary for ch. 2 (b) is very close to this: 'Who is God? Not in the first place an abstract belief in God, in his omnipotence etc. That is not a genuine experience of God, but a partial extension of the world.' Instead he talks of encounter with Jesus Christ. Then defines the experience of transcendence in a way that Paul would most certainly approve: 'The experience that a transformation of all human life is given in the fact that "Jesus is there for others" is explained as the experience of transcendence'.

Like Paul, Bonhoeffer has no static abstract idea of God or detached belief in God as omnipotent etc. Neither of them would have written the hymn:

Immortal, invisible, God only wise,
In light inaccessible hid from our eyes . . .
We blossom and flourish as leaves on the tree,
and wither and perish – but nought changeth thee.[17]

It is not that Paul would have disagreed with the hymn, but this is not what he sings about. He may at times have been caught up into the seventh heaven and seen visions which no one can describe. But this is not what he talks of as his genuine experience of God. It is his encounter with Jesus Christ and the experience of the Damascus road which left him blind and helpless until Christ opened his eyes to his mission. That mission is 'for others'. To the Jew first, for whom he was prepared to be damned if only they could encounter Christ; and for the Gentile, for whose liberty from the law he battled. Let Paul be our guide into the next chapter.

6

THE NON-RELIGIOUS INTERPRETATION
OF BIBLICAL CONCEPTS

In a non-religious world, the message of the gospel can only be understood if it is in non-religious terms. This transformation must be accomplished without losing the message of the gospel. There are dangers here, and the believer is quite right to be suspicious, to be angry at times, and often to cry, 'Blasphemy!' There were true believers who said this of Jesus, and also of St Paul in his time. How are we to distinguish those who have trivialised away the gospel message, or compromised it, from those who with confident faith try to speak the language of their day and often venture out of their depth? One is reminded of the wise words of D. T. Niles, the Methodist leader from Sri Lanka, when he was chairman of the Department of Evangelism of the World Council of Churches: 'You cannot evangelise without getting so close to the unbeliever that you are in danger of losing your own faith.'

I can still recall the agonising appeal of Josef Hromadka, when he was accused at the height of the Cold War of compromising his faith by working with a communist government in Czechoslovakia. John Foster Dulles had called him a fellow-traveller, who had betrayed his Christian faith. Hromadka responded by paying tribute to the martyrs who could do no other than oppose and die. 'But we', he said, 'are attempting the most difficult task of our lives. For the first time in our history, we have to learn how to witness to Jesus Christ in a state which professes atheism.' He appealed to those of us who had known him in the days before the war to trust him.

The church has traditionally poured scorn upon those who have tried to tell the gospel message in ways other than religious. In the First World War, poets and hymnwriters responded to the widespread tragedies of young men dying in their hundreds of thousands for their country, by calling them 'lesser Calvaries'. The dogmatist cried heresy, the theologians proclaimed the difference and the church, on the whole, disapproved. But many families learnt by that heretical phrase to bring their agonies to the foot of the cross – and some understood the sacrifice of our Lord much better. The high-sounding religious explanations had not touched them, but the agony of sacrifice in the brutality of war brought them nearer to the cross.

In more recent years, a controversial film, *The Last Temptation of Christ*, has brought forth cries of 'blasphemy' again. The naked Jesus, beaten up by the brutal soldiery, was so far removed from the Renaissance paintings of 'Christ at the Pillar' that it offended. And yet the reality was much nearer to that film version than to the painting. It was not a metaphysical Son of God who was scourged, but the man, Jesus of Nazareth. The novel by Nikos Kazantzakis[1] (and it is a work of fiction, with no pretension to historical accuracy), upon which the film was based, tried to understand, in a way that a religionless world might understand, the great biblical concepts of incarnation, atonement, sacrifice, *etc*. The film cannot be shown to those under eighteen, and it has already offended many devout believers. I suspect the offence has been mostly to do with the crude portrayal of nakedness and of Jesus, in fantasy, making love to a woman. All this is in the book, but the scenes do not appear there with such prominence.

Kazantzakis deals with many biblical concepts – and let us remember that he is a believer and is well aware of the sacredness of the concepts he handles. There are two issues dealt with that bring out the meaning of incarnation, atonement and sacrifice. The first issue is the relationship between Jesus and Judas. Judas is portrayed as very close to Jesus, even supporting him when he is doubtful about his destiny. As in Dennis Potter's earlier TV play: '*Son of Man*' (far more closely based upon the gospels than Kazantzakis), Jesus is shown as doubtful – the temptations and Gethsemane are illustrations and are brought close together. Both writers show Jesus aware of the alternative – perhaps he is after all just a man and is free to live the life of a man. Judas persuades him that he is the Messiah, and insists upon him going on with it.

In this relationship Jesus confesses the confusion in his mind when he feels like a man and speaks like God. Jesus has to choose death, and the only way is for Judas, his closest disciple, to betray him. In this fictional account it is Jesus who persuades him that he must do this. Judas is thus involved in the agony of choice. This agony of choice, which is the second issue, is brought out for Jesus in Gethsemane, and the ultimate decision to accept death. But Kazantzakis does not leave the doubts and uncertainties once Gethsemane is over. They continue even on the cross. And with a brilliance which has not a shred of historical evidence to support it, but which is a work of imagination, he describes the choice that Jesus makes. There is an alternative way. The rabbis show him the way: 'Come down from the cross.' Suppose he had not gone to the cross? His mind is set working on the alternative he has rejected. He dreams of the happiness of an ordinary family life – a woman he loves, marriage, children, responsibility, the joys of work. And in that mood he meets St Paul on Mars' Hill in Athens, with his little boy by his side. And as Paul is arguing the meaning of sacrifice, he looks on and listens, and says: 'No! It was not like this at all.'

Just as in the Judas scene, where Jesus argues that only by this betrayal can God and man be brought together, so in this fanciful scene on Mars' Hill, the clarity of the choice is shown. Incarnation means a real man; atonement is achieved through agony, both of God and man, Jesus and Judas; sacrifice is a real and terrible choice, which has an attractive alternative.

Neither this film, with all its offences, nor the brilliant novel of Kazantzakis offers us an acceptable way; but the reaction of the Greek Orthodox Church in excommunicating Kazantzakis, and of the Anglo-Saxon Christians who denounced the film as blasphemy, shows us the dangers which beset anyone who attempts to give a non-religious interpretation to the biblical concepts. Beware! The Inquisition has not entirely lost its sting.

CREATION

The controversy which rumbles on between creationists and evolutionists is not about the evidence or about details of the theory, but about the nature of knowledge. For the creationist, we know about creation by revelation. He will of course be glad to uncover defects in the theory of evolution, or produce evidence to show that it is faulty. But his main objection is about the nature of knowledge. He knows, because the truth has been revealed to him. He does not accept the world as it is or the conclusions of scientific investigations if they contradict what is made known to him in the scripture, which is the Word of God and therefore true. Science may uncover truths about God and creation, but they must be matched by God's own revelation. The text of the Bible may be discussed, and every effort made to discover what it really says, but what it says is true. Hence those who cannot accept the verbal inspiration of the Bible are quite unable to accept the creationist's conclusions without further evidence. The evolutionist depends upon observation and scientific analysis.

The difference is not about whether or not God created the world, but about how we know what he did and by what process it came into being. God spoke, says the creationist; God brought the world into being by a natural process which can be discovered or even, perhaps one day, observed, says the evolutionist. There are of course evolutionists who do not believe in God, but many do – and believe that he created all things, visible and invisible.

If we are to communicate the biblical concept of creation to a non-religious world, it is clear that we cannot do so by simply quoting the Bible. The world accepts that truth can be discovered, and the results of early work be corrected, by scientific methods. However, there is a growing humility among scientists themselves which is not always shared by the critics of religion, or by creationists. The issue of how to communicate the concept of creation to a non-religious world comes up more acutely and most profitably within the person who is both a scientist and a believer. Let me take as an example Charles Birch.[2]

Charles Birch

Like so many science students, the biologist Charles Birch was early dissatisfied with the orthodox Christianity in which he had been reared in Melbourne, Australia. He had gone to Adelaide to study biology, and was fascinated by the new world of scientific discovery. Many of his contemporaries left the church, considering it to be obscurantist and out-moded. The future belonged to science, and truth could be discovered by objective and unprejudiced research. But for Charles Birch, his church meant too much to him. He remained in a dilemma until at the crucial point someone introduced him to the writings of A. N. Whitehead. His comment twenty years later, looking back, was: 'I discovered something for myself that makes sense of the world of specialized knowledge in which I lived.'

What had worried him most was the impossible task of reconciling modern science with the idea of God interfering with his creation from outside. The work of Whitehead and Charles Hartshorne had helped him to see that a believer could discover God in the processes of the world. It was an exciting new discovery for him, which enabled him to pursue his scientific studies with an almost religious fervour! His biology had already awakened him to the need to discover something of the process of evolution. Now the story of creation became much more exciting. God was in it, not merely starting it off and interfering from time to time.

The young science student has since become one of the most distinguished biologists in the world and, as Professor Charles Birch, has lectured throughout the world. His close friendship with Dr Theodosius Dobzhansky has helped him to develop his philosophy of science. It has also led him to campaign for a proper use of nature in an ecological cause. In this he takes his stance upon God's requirement of humans that they should 'replenish the earth'. The fact that he can quote from Genesis in his defence of 'the green planet' does not commit him to a literal understanding of how things began according to Genesis 1 or Genesis 2. He is satisfied that he can talk to his fellow scientists and to others about God's creation in terms of the evolutionary process. In the Camden Lectures that he gave in Sydney in 1964,[3] he summarised his position:

Creation is the concrete realization of what is potentially possible in the universe;
Creation is the lifting of restraints on matter;
In creation, the creature becomes more aware with every creative advance;
Creation is the reaction of the world upon God as well as the action of God upon the world;
Creation is the unity of nature in God; God who is creator is also redeemer.

His Camden Lectures represent the beginning of Birch's attempt to describe creation and the creative process in terms which required God and yet were more intelligible to non-religious people. Of course, he developed over the years. Just as science also developed. In the ten years following the Camden Lectures, much progress had been made in identifying the elementary mechanisms of evolution, the genetic code had been cracked and Jacques Monod had published his *Chance and Necessity*. Monod attacked Christians and Marxists alike for postulating purpose in the universe. He maintained that biology was now sufficiently advanced to say that chance and necessity explained everything. Nature reproduced accurately if unimaginatively. What we called progress was the occasional accidental change which was then accurately reproduced. This guarantees neither improvement nor purpose. The controversy raged, and Birch joined in with a paper which he delivered in Mexico to the Faith and Order Conference of the World Council of Churches. He attacked scientists and theologians alike: the scientist leaves no room for God in the world, while the theologian brings him in to do the wrong job! He averred: 'It is meaningless and hopelessly confusing to say that this or that physical or biological event occurs because God makes it happen that way.'

Charles Birch sought a theology which would contribute a dimension of understanding to what he found in biology. He was by now wedded to 'process theology', taking his lead from Charles Hartshorne. Like Bonhoeffer, Birch did not lose transcendence, but brought it down from its aloofness: God was in the process, immanent and yet transcendent. Science had also to be corrected, and he would not allow Jacques Monod to get away with a mechanistic view of the universe. The lower mechanical mode is wrongly used to explain the higher organism, but the reverse is true. Birch developed his thesis: Every human experience is based upon past experience and anticipates the future. Memory and anticipation are causes of present action. This he sees as one of the crucial elements in the mechanism of evolution, which even at its earliest stage must be explained in terms of the complexity to which it is moving. You do not seek to understand man by studying the lower animals, but you understand the lower animals as you uncover the mystery of humanity.

Like Teilhard de Chardin, Charles Birch looks at evolution in terms of purpose rather than in terms of origin. His model for creation comes from his study of the human organism. He maintains that there is a realm of possibilities in the universe which has a value structure. This is consonant with Paul Davies, who in *The Cosmic Blueprint*[4] went as far as to say that something seemed to be going on behind the process of the universe! According to Charles Birch, humanity moves forward, not with intrinsic values, nor does he or she create values, but appropriates them. Humanity has the experience of being able to choose. From that point, he argues, 'part of the implicit order of the universe is this realm of values which presses on us as possibilities from which we choose and are chosen. This is what we mean by the influence of God upon the human experience.'

Unlike Teilhardians and many Christians, Birch accepts most of Monod's arguments in *Chance and Necessity*, but his end picture is different. It is not Sisyphus pushing the stone up the hill only to let it fall back again. Monod's concluding paragraph read, 'The ancient covenant is in pieces; man at last knows that he is alone in the unfeeling immensity of the universe, out of which he emerged only by chance.'[5] For 'chance', Birch would read *choice*. And while he accepted the next sentence, 'Neither his destiny nor his duty are written down,' and even the apparently gloomy conclusion, 'The kingdom above or the darkness below; it is for him to choose,' Birch read it differently because he could not accept the 'unfeeling immensity'. Instead he saw love and feeling in the universe, because he saw God there. As with Monod, the choice is decisive, but it is a choice made in the universe of love, where the realm of values presses in upon us, where memory and anticipation play their part, and where God is in the whole process of memory, anticipation and choice: 'God is both the sustainer of existence and the lure of existence.'

This has not left Birch with a dead theory, but a living experience which breaks through in his very language: 'The world is not as tame as our sluggish, convention-ridden imaginations tend to suppose,' and 'Ordered development out of sheer potentials and spontaneity requires that there be love in the universe.' Such a view of the universe and of creation has come from his discovery of God in the very processes with which he was daily concerned in his scientific research. Birch has found a reason for the scientist to retain his faith without betraying his intellectual integrity, and for the believer to look with hope towards the unfolding processes of the universe. It has led him to be a champion of the earth, warning of the icebergs which our planet is in danger of striking if we continue to treat the earth as though it were meaningless matter for our exploitation.

Charles Birch is profoundly biblical in his view, which owes much to Paul's eighth chapter of his Epistle to the Romans. If we lay that text beside the Camden Lectures, with their summary points about God and creation, and the Mexico paper, with its dynamic relationship between theology and science, we shall recognise the kinship:

I consider that the sufferings of this present time are not worth comparing with the glory that is to be revealed to us. For the creation waits with eager longing for the revealing of the sons of God . . . because the creation itself will be set free from its bondage to decay and obtain the glorious liberty of the children of God. (Romans 8:18–21)

Charles Birch has not said the last word, but he has shown a way to talk of creation to a non-religious world.[6]

THE FALL

The biblical concept of the fall has been built upon by so much theology and traditional assumptions and practices that it is sometimes difficult to grasp what the Bible actually says about this concept. Like other creation myths, it tells of a state of perfection, remembered and longed for, in which humanity is in perfect harmony with nature and all living creatures – a green earth with ecological balance. The tragedy comes with the loss of that paradise because of an act of disobedience. Like all myths, it explains a deep-felt longing and fear, buried in the unconscious. The setting is a religious one, in which God is the benefactor and law-giver. Humanity, male and female, is totally dependent on God, and the relationship is undisturbed so long as no act of rebellion against his will is attempted. When the act of disobedience is perpetrated, then paradise collapses. The act of disobedience is linked with the relationship of the man to the woman. After the expulsion from Eden, God continues to watch over his creatures, but now in a sterner mood. The subsequent story tells that all is not well and only God can put it right.

If we follow Bultmann, we can demythologise that story and, as we interpret it, it resonates with meaning and finds an echo in our experience. We are aware that God created us to be the wardens of creation – 'fruitful and multiplying and replenishing the earth'. We are also aware that this should give us harmony with nature. Because we are not caring for the earth, but exploiting it, we are using nature instead of caring for it. We are disobedient. That disobedience comes from a desire to satisfy our own longing for pleasure. Further, the fact that male and female are both involved in the fall, indeed their coming together has made it possible, leads us to concentrate upon sex as the root of disobedience. This is further strengthened by the consequences of the fall, which began with a sense of shame. 'Who told you that you were naked?' (Genesis 3:11). The consequences continue with an estrangement from nature and a troubled and painful childbirth, the fruit of sex. This could lead us in our demythologising to interpret Genesis 2 and 3 as a longing for harmony with nature, which by some act of ours has become hostile to us, and a seeking for true satisfaction in sex. The search is fruitless on both scores unless God lead us back to Eden. The drama of salvation is then the story of how God restores us to sinless, obedient children. The myth has been interpreted and the mythological material removed.

But, for Bonhoeffer, that does not go far enough. We must remove the religious structure with which the mythological is inseparably intertwined. This would lead us to turn away from the absolute character of revelation (Bonhoeffer's criticism of Barth) and listen to what the scientists have discovered about our nature. Can we find, then, an equivalent to the fall in the discoveries of those who have explored the mind?

Sigmund Freud, developing the concept of the unconscious, found experiences there which had been forgotten. In particular, he explained neurosis in later life as due to the oedipus complex in childhood: the early desire of the child to break the double taboo – desiring the mother in a sexual relationship and hating the father as a rival who should be killed. Melanie Klein took this further back, to show the child's love and hatred of the mother – the source of all goodness and yet the tyrant who can withhold that goodness. The desire to attack the mother, or rather attack the 'bad breast', is a source of neurosis until uncovered and understood. Carl Gustav Jung, fearful of Freud's overconcentration on sex, explored his own unconscious and later developed a concept of universal archetypes in the unconscious of all humanity. Bruno Bettelheim has discovered in the telling of fairy stories and the classical myths something which corresponds to the memory of all people.

Others have explored the unconscious in other ways. But what seems to be universal is something which happens in all of us at an early age, of which later we are ashamed. It is in the opinion of most psychologists to do with sex and assertiveness, unbridled pleasure and selfishness. It disturbs a dream of perfection and peace which is our 'lost Eden' and if not accepted can become so painful as to be neurotic and lead to an estrangement from nature and other people. This is a sickness that needs treatment. The psychiatrists will help the client to face up to early experience and the sense of shame. A Freudian will hope to remove the harmful effect of repression by bringing it out into the open. Viktor Frankl, in what he calls 'logotherapy', is not content with releasing the repression, but seeks to help the client discover a purpose in life. An Adlerian will follow similar lines on the basis of rather different theories. Bruno Bettelheim, himself a Freudian, will deal with the resistance to shame by acceptance and love. There are great varieties, but the one constant thing in all psychological theories is that something has happened which can be related to what the Christian means by the fall.

All therapists agree that the harmful effects of repressing this event or attitude need treatment, and that the situation can be treated by a form of liberation. In Freud's own day, Oscar Pfister, a Protestant pastor in Switzerland, made good use of Freud's theories in his pastoral work. If we simply oppose the many psychological theories and psychotherapeutic practices, we are ignoring a whole world of understanding. We then go on talking about the fall in terms that have no meaning in a non-religious world. Psychology has given to us a tool with which to understand and communicate the biblical concept of the fall.

ATONEMENT

The traditional explanation of the Atonement is that it concerns the reconciliation of humanity with God, a reconciliation made necessary by the human estrangement due to the fall. The Atonement is the healing of the separation, and it is seen as done from God's side. How is by no means clear. There have been various theories of the atonement. The fall has made us unable to approach God, for whom we are created, and in his purity God cannot come near to sin. This is akin to the Greek idea that the gods cannot be present when a human dies! But the Christian theory of 'substitution' follows the Hebrew idea of purification. As an animal was killed and sacrificed as an 'atonement' for sin, so the perfect sacrifice has to be the perfect person. We should die for our sin. Adam was warned of this. God demands a sacrifice, and he accepts the sacrifice of his own Son. Thus we are reconciled to God not because we have been made righteous, but pleading his righteousness.

There are other theories. One is that the cross is a triumph over the evil that enthralls us. *Christus Victor* overcomes sin and death – for us. Another is that on the cross God is involved, and through the suffering of his Son appeals to us.

This whole complex is religious talk, unintelligible to a non-religious world. Before we can begin to tackle the interpretation of the concept we must go back and clarify what we mean by 'God' and how we shall talk of God to a non-religious world. Bonhoeffer certainly found it easier to talk of God to unbelievers (and not with the purpose of converting them) than he did with Christians. What then have we said of God which would enable us to talk of atonement?

Bonhoeffer's theology is concerned to the end with Feuerbach's unanswered questions about God. As early as 1931, in his first Berlin lecture, Bonhoeffer said: 'Feuerbach put two questions to theology which remain unanswered: the first concerns the truth of its proposition (i.e. to be able to speak about God); the second, its relevance to real life.'

Feuerbach asked the questions implying the denial of any authenticity or truth in faith. For him there was no God, and the image of God created by faith was irrelevant. Bonhoeffer wrestled with those questions with the conviction of faith, seeking to establish the authenticity of the Christian proclamation.

Barth had attempted this systematically in his *The Humanity of God*, but he was cautious and did not take the risks that Bonhoeffer did. As Eberhard Bethge says: 'Bonhoeffer risked more, throwing himself almost exclusively on to Christology. He stepped nearer, dangerously nearer, the theological abyss and set more in motion than either Barth or Feuerbach ever did. But I would not say, as some people do, that he has taken us into the abyss.'[7]

This almost exclusively Christological approach to God meant the end of any view of God as a new power-structure. It was the God with scars whom Bonhoeffer saw. He threw away Feuerbach's taunt that God appeared to be an unapproachable despot to whom man must be sacrificed. He emphasised the God who sacrificed himself that man might live. Henry Mottu encapsulates it in a short sentence: 'The token sign of the non-religious God is actually his weakness, not his exploitation of my weakness.'[8]

Bonhoeffer's approach goes further than Whitehead, whose God of persuasive love influences and is influenced by the world, and allows 'freedom in man and spontaneity in nature'. Philip Toynbee, in his autobiographical journal *Part of a Journey*, shows how inadequate Whitehead is:

> But not even this [Whitehead's God of persuasive love, *etc.*] gets away from the problem of omnipotence; therefore the problem of evil. For if God allows spontaneity in nature, but could control it if he wished, then he is just as much responsible for earthquakes as if he had planned each one of them.[9]

Toynbee, emerging from his years of deep depression, indicates the kind of God he could speak of with a sense of truth and relevance:

> I'd prefer to speak of a God who enables man to be partially free within his natural environment of iron necessity. And I see God confronting the natural world not as his creation, but the given material with which he has to work on earth. Or the given domain within which he has to work. God/Heaven forever striving to penetrate Man/Earth. (But Man and Earth are appallingly resistant to the offered light and freedom).[10]

He confesses in another part of his journal that for many years he was prevented from making that journey towards faith in God 'by my revulsion against the Omnipotent God of Christian orthodoxy'. There are many like him, and it is to this multitude that we as believers must tell of a God of persuasive love.

We have already seen Bonhoeffer's key concept of God as 'being there for others'. This has put a limitation on his omnipotence as usually considered, just as love limits omnipotence. The metaphysical question as to whether God can be both omnipotent and loving is an irrelevant question. The self-limiting of Jesus Christ illustrates this. Not only in Philippians 2 is he seen as 'emptying himself'. And if we move on to the Christological emphasis, which is all that we can know of God, certainly what we know of God revealed in Jesus Christ has little to do with omnipotence.

Those who pull out the miracles from the gospels to contemplate as a new power-structure, a return of the *deus ex machina*, 'to heal all our diseases', have left behind the essence of the gospel. Jesus of Nazareth 'went about doing good', brought joy to a wedding feast, taught forgiveness to the utmost, seventy times seven, touched the leper and was not afraid of the deranged; he was the man who loved the unlovely. All this is our picture of God. He healed the sick, gave sight to the blind, encouraged the outcasts and cared for sinners. There was no demonstration of omnipotence. No legions of angels came to save him when threatened with death. He died, and no power from heaven stopped the cruel death. God raised him from the dead, not to punish his enemies, whom he had already forgiven, but to send a band of disciples into all the world to tell of God's love and bring them into his kingdom.

If this is the kind of God with whom we have to deal, then the atonement can only be an act of love. It cannot be a despot demanding sacrifice. God is on the side of humanity. Reading the gospels does not convince us that he is on the side of religion, but most certainly on the side of suffering, sinful, arrogant humanity. And he loves them while they are yet in their sins. There is no indication that he is like a Victorian father who only sees his children when they have been washed and scrubbed and properly dressed in clean clothes.

Atonement is the essential love of God for humanity. It has to do with the larger areas of life, not only individuals who have seen the light. It is the world that God loves, with all its dirt and sin. He asked only that we believe what Jesus Christ shows and tells of the Father. If we may paraphrase Augustine: 'His heart is restless, until ours rests in his.' The three parables that fill the fifteenth chapter of Luke's gospel tell of a shepherd who looks for a sheep, a woman who seeks a piece of silver and a father who waits for a lost son. They all three are parables of the atonement. They tell of God's search until he finds. And it is not one or two chosen souls for whom he searches, but humanity. The kingdom of God, better translated as the rule of God, is his gentle rule over all mankind. 'His yoke is easy and his burden light.' Can we not see God's persuasive love winning mankind by his weakness, his suffering and his readiness to be for us?

REPENTANCE

Traditionally, we have tended to put repentance into a model pattern. Confess, repent, receive forgiveness, then you are saved. There is much in the gospels to call that pattern in question. The woman taken in adultery is forgiven, although no repentance is recorded. Jesus calls Zacchaeus down from the tree before any profession of repentance. John the Baptist preached repentance and demanded 'fruits worthy of repentance', but although Jesus took up the theme, and the early church told those who were convicted of their sins to repent, the overwhelming impression of the way Jesus dealt with sinners was that of taking the initiative of love. He called upon God to forgive his persecutors who showed no sign of repentance. So how shall we talk to a non-religious world about repentance?

It has two religious connotations: first in the practice of confession, a disciplined scouring of the past in which repentance is in danger of becoming a routine; and secondly in conversion or sudden 'salvation', in which past sins are obliterated at a single swoop of heavenly grace.

Philip Toynbee, in his journal *Part of a Journey*, sought to find an alternative word to retain the meaning without the religious connotations. He tried, in turn, *reorientation*, clumsy, but as he said 'I like the implication of turning towards the rising sun'; *rebirth*, too special; *salvation*, 'has that horrid ring of a spiritual arrogance'; *amendment*, good, but something bolder is needed; *renewal*, the best so far, 'suggesting both a process and the possibility of sudden change'.[11] This searching is for a word that would break out of the narrow religious framework. Whatever word we use, it is necessary to be quite clear what we are talking about.

Perhaps John the Baptist gives us a clue. He called for repentance in preparation for the future. And he wanted more than words: 'Bring forth fruits worthy of repentance.' He did not hesitate to itemise those fruits – do violence to no man; be content with your wages; he who has two coats share with him who has none; and, to tax-collectors, collect no more than is due. He knew the nature of phoney repentance. All the words that Philip Toynbee uses are attempts to grasp the forward-looking nature of 'repentance'. It is a state of mind in which one recognises that things are not right. 'Get right with God' is a call to repentance; but also to 'know thyself'. It is an honest assessment of one's failed condition and a determination to turn round and change. A believer is convinced that God helps a person to do this. And this change is neither an emotional state nor a temporary condition, it is a change towards the future.

This is well summed up in a familiar quotation: 'God grant me the courage to change the things I can change; the serenity to accept those I cannot change; and the wisdom to know the difference.' There are very few who are not constantly in need of repentance in order to enter the future 'unstained by the past', and there are some who will find it in a flash of enlightenment which makes it easier to go forward. Repentance is a gift of God to those in need of help to pull themselves out of the consequences of the past.

FAITH

In his booklet *The Difference in Being a Christian Today*, John Robinson quotes an article in the *Daily Mail* (5 December 1970) by Peter Lewis, in which he says of the Pope and the Archbishop of Canterbury that they appeared to be 'two elderly and puzzled men . . . who no longer represent anything but doubt and confusion'. At first, John Robinson says, he thought this was another snide and negative jibe at the church. But when he read the whole article he saw that Lewis was taking doubt seriously as an ingredient of faith. The article returns to the subject of doubt towards the end: 'The religion that survives, if any does, is going to have to be a religion of doubt . . . A new human idea of God is struggling to be born. When that changes all must change with it, however fiercely people bid the waves retreat.'[12]

John Bowden, in his *Jesus: The Unanswered Questions*, points out that such changes took place within the New Testament itself. And not necessarily for the good! Christianity moved at an early stage from looking forward to the return of Christ in the immediate future, to looking back to Christ as the centre. The first followers may have been mistaken about the return of Christ, but surely they were right in looking forward rather than backwards. Bowden concludes: 'Faith must always be an ongoing quest into new territory, supported by the expectation that there is always more to learn and discover.'[13]

Philip Toynbee in his quest also found himself discovering old and forgotten truths before venturing into new territories. After attending evensong in Peterborough Cathedral, he concluded that if the faith which is now dying among us is to be reborn it will need to shine at least as brightly as the splendid and inspiring liturgy produced by the full array of orthodox Christian doctrine![14]

Every new exploration of Christian doctrine must turn back to the New Testament, where the sources lie for a new understanding of faith. This generation can approach the old documents with experiences others have not had, and with an understanding of truth which is refined by scientific research.

This is not to make faith materialistic, or to dispose of transcendence or the spiritual dimension. It is to look with fresh eyes, with a slight shift of vision that might, as Toynbee says, 'reilluminate the word and give a new Christian message to our time'.[15] To do this we need to look at the Old and New Testaments in the light of our modern historical perspective. For, although it is true, as Alasdair MacIntyre says, that 'everything of importance to religious faith is outside the reach of historical investigation',[16] it is also true that our generation must look at the development of faith in historical terms.

Thus the God of the Old Testament is seen as a developing God, because we detect a growing understanding of faith, influenced by historical events and growing perception. The earliest writings in the Old Testament show faith in a God who is seen as some great king or emperor who is able to deliver out of the hands of all enemies. The historical event of the Exodus from Egypt confirmed this. The long trek across the wilderness, which seems characteristic of many religions, was told as evidence of God's power to heal all their diseases. The earliest beliefs seem to have been of some powerful tribal tyrant who was good to those who obeyed him, but terrifying to those who broke his commandments. The lines begin to soften even as early as Hosea in the eighth century BC. In the fifth century BC Jeremiah is talking of a new kind of relationship with this God, one that is not accompanied by awesome rituals, but direct:

> I will put my law within them, and I will write it upon their hearts; and I will be their God, and they shall be my people . . . they shall all know me, from the least of them to the greatest . . . for I will forgive their iniquity, and I will remember their sin no more. (Jeremiah 31:33–34)

The God whom Jesus proclaimed and taught his followers to call 'Father' in familiar terms was almost a new vision of God. He did not totally dispense with what went before, but uncovered new beauties. Philip Toynbee's description of the God Jesus asked us to believe in is well phrased: 'like a sublime statue half emerging from a great block of rough hewn granite'.[17] In what is preserved of the teaching of Jesus it is quite clear that he intended this vision of God to grow. He recognised the limitations of his disciples. There were things he could not share with them because they were not ready.

Neither was he without doubts. The story of the temptations show his wrestling with the nature of his mission, depending upon the vision of the Father. His answers to the temptations are all taken from the Old Testament, and the temptations themselves come from this earlier view of God – God the provider of bread for the hungry by miraculous means, like manna in the wilderness; God the miracle-worker, upholding his favourite Son lest he dash his foot against a stone; God the ruler of the world. The all-powerful God, like some emperor of unheard power, is rejected by Jesus. Gethsemane is also a time of doubt and struggle. Yet the traditional God of Christianity has become the same old emperor who appeared in the earliest sources of Hebrew writing, softened now by love. This tribal tyrant now loves his creatures as a father loves his children. And thereby an insoluble problem has been presented to faith. How can God be all-powerful, hence responsible for everything that happens, and still be regarded as all-loving? The floods in Bangladesh, the famine in Africa, earthquakes, cyclones: is he a God who weeps, or a mysterious power who has some obscure reason for letting this happen? There is no doubt that Jesus would have opted for the father who weeps. The new vision of God which seems to emerge in our day when we look with our eyes and our experience of the Bible is of a God who does not possess two distinct attributes called 'power' and 'love', but a God whose power lies only and wholly in his love.

THE NEW LIFE

'If any one is *in Christ*, he is *a new creation*' (2 Corinthians 5:17). The claim of 'new life' which is central to the Christian understanding of 'conversion' has to be explained as well as justified. In his *Ethics*, Bonhoeffer begins his discussion of 'new life'[18] by relating it to 'good'. He does this on the basis of certain texts in the Fourth Gospel.[19]

First there is the Prologue, which claims for the *Logos* (which became flesh and dwelt among us), the source of all creation: 'all things were made through him, and without him was not anything made that was made' (John 1:3). Then in the next verse, 'In him was life, and the life was the light of men' (John 1:4). He couples with this the claim recorded as by Jesus himself: '*I am* the way, and the truth, and *the life*' (John 14:6). This claim of Jesus is taken to mean much more than '*I am the life*', as though he might be some principle imposed upon all living things, but that he is 'my life', 'our life'. Paul spells this out in more than one letter: 'For to me to live is Christ' (Philippians 1:21); 'When Christ who is our life appears . . .' (Colossians 3:4). But this clearly is not a description of the life of believers only. For this *life* was the light of men, further defined as, 'The true light that enlightens every man' (John 1:9). This is revelation, that our life is outside ourselves and in Jesus Christ. We do not learn that from experience or observation. We can believe it or contradict it. If we believe it, we recognise that we have fallen away, 'from life, from our life, and that we are living in contradiction to life, to our life'.[20]

It is perhaps helpful to note the context in which Jesus is reported as saying, '*I am . . . the life*'. It is in the farewell discourses, when he is explaining that he is to leave them. Peter has already made his protest and insisted that he will follow Jesus through death if needs be. 'Not yet', says Jesus, and then seeks to encourage them. He is merely going ahead of them to prepare a place for them, where they can be with him forever. He adds, 'Where I am going you know, and the way you know' (John 14:4). Thomas does not know and wants to know: 'Lord, we do not know where you are going; how can we know the way?' (John 14:5). The following verse closely identifies Christ with the Father and makes the claim, 'I am . . . the life': 'I am the way, and the truth, and the life; no one comes to the Father, but by me. If you had known me, you would have known my Father also; henceforth, you know him and have seen him' (John 14:7).

The context is death – the death of Jesus and the future death of the disciples. Jesus insists that, although they and we are living lives which contradict 'our life', he is still 'our life'. Ours is the negation; his is the affirmation.

> This negation of our apostate life means that between it and the life which is in Jesus Christ there stands the end, annihilation, death . . . But in bringing us death this 'no' becomes a mysterious 'yes', the affirmation of a new life, the life which is Jesus Christ. This is the life that we cannot give to ourselves, the life that comes to us entirely from without, entirely from beyond; and yet it is not a remote or alien life, of no concern to ourselves, but it is our own real daily life. This life lies hidden only behind the symbol of death, the symbol of negation.[21]

Here Bonhoeffer is very close to Bultmann, particularly in the latter's *Commentary on John*.

If we cannot deduce this from observation, nor confirm it except in subjective experience, such as Paul uses in personal testimony, we can explain it in non-religious terms. We can observe alienation. Karl Marx has expounded this at great length in his early writings. He has many examples of how a rich person can acquire the character he chooses by virtue of his wealth. He has the power of the horses he can purchase, or we would say, the car he drives. In fact, we are more aware than Marx was of the psychological mechanism of alienation. For many people, their own life is outside of them. What they live is not their true life, their own life. There is a restlessness, seeking to be oneself.

The Christian message is that there is a way to be oneself, and this is, in fact, the new life which the Bible speaks of. It is acquired by recognising it in Jesus Christ and accepting it. It is at this point that the importance of associating the 'new life' with the 'good' is crucial to Bonhoeffer's *Ethics*. He does not accept an ethic which is imposed from outside, but one that is recognised as one's own. In the language of the prophets, it is a move from the old covenant of obedience to the law, to the new covenant of the law written in the heart. The appeal, then, to 'accept Christ' or to 'get right with God' is not an appeal to change into someone else, but to become oneself. The lifestyle is then to become conformed with Christ.

Paul explains this clearly in Romans 12. He appeals to his largely unknown readers to offer their bodies like a living sacrifice. But then he goes on to say: 'Do not be conformed to this world' (Romans 12:2), which J. B. Phillips has rightly translated, 'Don't let the world around you squeeze you into its own mould . . .' Christians do not receive new life like a mould, shaping them according to a predestined pattern. But rather, are to 'be transformed by the renewal of your mind'. That is not being shaped, but being renewed. And renewal from within, the renewal of the mind, is becoming what we really are.

New life is the breaking through of the original, like a dammed up river finding its own river bed. The change may be violent or gradual. The result is the same: living one's own life, not imitating another's. And this is acquired as we recognise that Christ is our life. The life that we have desired has all along been our own, but we have lived a false life, negating our true life, until he offers his yes to our no, and new life flows in. Thus we become ourselves.

THE LAST THINGS

The Advent season has traditionally been the time when the church took a look at what were called 'the last things', four in all: death, judgement, heaven and hell.

No religion or philosophy which attempts to provide a view of life can ignore the inevitable experience of death, but these 'four last things' have put death into a mythological framework. The framework is derived from the contemporary Judaism within which Jesus naturally cast his teaching, and was much elaborated in the Middle Ages, adding purgatory to soften the hard distinction between heaven and hell, and was immortally described by Dante in his *Divine Comedy*.

The four last things belong to what Bonhoeffer refers to in his letter of the 8 June 1944.[22] They are what the church still stands guard over:

Efforts are made to prove to a world thus come of age that it cannot live without the tutelage of 'God'. Even though there has been surrender on all secular problems, there still remain the so-called 'ultimate questions' – death, guilt – to which only 'God' can give an answer, and because of which we need God and the church and the pastor.[23]

He is dissatisfied with this peripheral role, and asks the further question: 'But what if one day they [*i.e.* the ultimate questions] no longer exist as such, if they too can be answered "without God"?'

1 Death

There is no question about 'death'. It is inevitable, and no scientist seriously believes that science can do more than postpone it. The question concerns the attitude to death and the consciousness that follows it for the individual or the community. The serious attention paid to death and to the rites of passage associated with it goes back into remote antiquity. It is one of the unique characteristics of the human race that death should be accompanied by a special rite of disposal. In the New Testament, death is almost always associated with resurrection. This is linked with the resurrection of Jesus from the dead, a crucial part of the Christian proclamation (and the earliest, according to Acts 2). The fate of those who died believing was intertwined with the resurrection.

Paul deals with this most clearly to assure those Christians who had expected Christ's early return and were troubled by the death of their fellow believers before he came. In a classic passage, 1 Corinthians 15, he gives evidence for the resurrection of Christ – quoting all the examples he knows of resurrection appearances, adding his own experience of the risen Christ. He assures his readers that the resurrection of Christ is an essential part of the Christian proclamation. And our resurrection is dependent upon that. So to deny that the dead are raised is equivalent to denying the truth of the gospel.

Basically, then, what is said about life after death is that it is dependent upon a relationship with Christ. The Fourth Gospel describes Christ's death as a journey ahead of his disciples, preparing the way. They will eventually die, but they are not to regard this as a tragedy. It is a passage from one form of existence to another.

On the basis of the New Testament witness, then, we can talk of death as a part of life which must be taken seriously, but not tragically. It does not represent loss, but growth. If a person were only physical, and everything about him or her could be explained in physical terms, then death is simply the end. The physical decomposes after death. But if the person is more than physical, then that which is more survives. Many scientific tests and pseudo-scientific tests have sought to show that there is survival after death. There is no reason to quarrel with that as a piece of evidence; but it does not tell you much. Mere survival is hardly good news. If an old person, weary of life, was told that he or she would survive, and nothing more, it would be bad news!

What we have to say on the basis of the resurrection of Christ is that there are qualities of human life that develop after death, free from the limitations of human frailty as we know it. That continuance depends upon a living relationship which cannot be destroyed by death. Death has a limited victory over the human person, and what it conquers and destroys is merely the physical limitation of a personality, destined to progress in a larger consciousness beyond death. More cannot be said. The curtain of death hides a mystery, but those who have known Christ in their lives are assured that they will know him still after death.

2 Judgement

The teaching of Jesus, as recorded in the gospels, contains a great deal about separation, and many parables talk of separating wheat from tares, wise from foolish, sheep from goats, *etc*. The fullest account of this teaching is in the extended parable of the last judgement in Matthew 25:31–46. It takes place on the return of Christ in glory. All the parables of separation indicate that the differences will be revealed when the Lord returns. In this passage, the 'Christ for others' is emphasised to such an extent that Christ is the person in need whom the righteous serve without identifying, and the unrighteous fail to serve because they have not identified the Christ in the brother who is sick or in prison, hungry or naked. The distinction between those who are at home with Christ and those who are rejected is in terms of attitudes taken during their daily life. Tares and wheat are allowed to grow together until the harvest, foolish virgins are careless of the need to prepare, the righteous and the unrighteous are judged by the attitude they have to the poor. There is nothing very religious about these distinctions. All of them, in fact, say that ultimately there is a judgement made which affects eternity, but which is made already before death, whether you know it or not. We have to convey in this biblical concept that what we do and how we relate to others in this life is of eternal significance and influences the kind of life we live beyond death in that larger consciousness.

3 Heaven

The Bible says very little about heaven until it gets to the Book of Revelation. Then the symbolism is so complex that it is dangerous to conclude that we know anything about the details! Hebrews and Revelation are both full of images. Many are mythological – a city with gates and huge precious stones, rivers and trees giving fruit all the year round, no night, no sea to separate, no temple but the overwhelming presence of Christ in glory. This is the imagination bursting out on all sides, declaring everything dreamt of and desired as fulfilled in heaven. More simply, Hebrews talks of a city whose builder and maker is God.

After reading the most elaborate passages in Revelation one concludes that heaven is not a place but a state of consciousness. In the last judgement parable, it is simply 'inherit the kingdom prepared for you from the foundation of the world' (Matthew 25:34). In our present secular society, with all the knowledge we have gained of the universe, it is as foolish to search for heaven among the stars as to look for the soul in the body. But a Christian believer is convinced that there is life – or a consciousness which we can only talk of as life – beyond death. And it is an enlargement of our consciousness, to be anticipated with joy or even longing.

That attitude of longing to be with the Lord is characteristic of much in the New Testament writings, and is described particularly by Paul in the chapter already quoted:

> Lo! I tell you a mystery. We shall not all sleep, but we shall all be changed, in a moment, in the twinkling of an eye, at the last trumpet. For the trumpet will sound, and the dead will be raised imperishable, and we shall be changed. For this perishable nature must put on the imperishable, and this mortal nature must put on immortality. (1 Corinthians 15:51–53)

Not much more can be said to a believer. The last stanza of Bonhoeffer's poem 'Stations on the Road to Freedom'[24] can talk of death as 'thou greatest of feasts on the journey to freedom eternal'. This is 'heaven' as we can describe it today: 'casting aside all the burdensome chains', 'demolishing the walls of our temporal bodies . . . of our souls that are blinded'. It is then that we 'see that which here remains hidden.'

4   Hell

There has to be an alternative! Man's imagination has been used richly, but not very profitably, in trying to think of the nastiest things to put in hell. This was perhaps understandable when the Christians were being cruelly persecuted. They had very natural desires to revenge themselves on their persecutors. But Jesus did not encourage that kind of thinking. We may have to demythologise even the words attributed to him in Matthew 25:41: 'Depart from me, you cursed, into the eternal fire prepared for the devil and his angels' . . . Perhaps he too had moments when, seeing the injustice done to the poor, he was angry at the aggressors. The film, *The Last*

Temptation of Christ wrestles with this and makes Jesus say, 'When they persecuted Mary Magdalene, I wanted to kill them, but only words of love came out.' Those words are also in Nikos Kazantzakis' book. They recall the God portrayed in Hosea, who envisages punishing his rebellious people by sending them back to slavery in Egypt or to Assyria, and then repents:

> How, oh how, can I give you up, Ephraim!
> How, oh how, can I hand you over, Israel!
> How can I turn you into a Sodom!
> How can I treat you like a Gomorrah!
> My heart recoils within me,
> All my compassion is kindled.
> I will not give vent to my fierce anger –
> I will not destroy Ephraim again.
> For I am God and not man,
> I am the Holy One in your very midst,
> And I have not come to destroy.
> (Hosea 11:8–9, J. B. Phillips' translation)[25]

With such a God it is better not to be too precise about hell. To talk of the furniture of heaven or the temperature of hell is to court disaster and make fools of ourselves in the presence of a forgiving God. We may find it difficult to be as forgiving as God or to believe that all will be saved. Jürgen Moltmann, when asked if he were a 'universalist' in this sense of all being saved from this terrible alternative, said, 'No!' But he added, 'I sometimes suspect that God is!' It is not profitable to dwell upon eternal punishment of the wicked, and hell has no real place in our Christian proclamation. It is, after all, not the will of our Father that anyone should perish.

The Justification of the Sinner by Grace Alone

But is that what Bonhoeffer meant by 'the last things' in his list of biblical concepts? He may have done, and certainly we have to talk about these four last things which have become so stereotyped in popular presentations of Christianity. However, he used the phrase in a different sense in his *Ethics*.

The most compact piece of theological writing gathered in that collection of studies, whose order constantly puzzles us, is called 'The Last Things and the Things Before the Last'.[26] It was composed in the monastery in Ettal, between the end of November 1940 and the middle of February 1941, when Bonhoeffer broke off to go to Switzerland. Its key phrase was also used earlier. It is very much a piece of Reformation study, and its influence runs through all he wrote about ethics and the Christian way of life.

For Bonhoeffer, the origin and essence of all Christian life is comprised in the one process, which since the Reformation we have called, 'justification of the sinner by grace alone'. The totality of life is contained in this event, and Bonhoeffer describes it vividly:

> It is something final, something which cannot be grasped by the being or the action or the suffering of any man. The dark pit of human life, inwardly and outwardly barred, sinking ever more hopelessly and inescapably in the abyss, is torn open by main force, and the word of God breaks in. In the rescuing light man for the first time recognizes God and his neighbour. The labyrinth of the life he has so far led falls in ruin. Man is free for God and his brothers.[27]

There is no difficulty in finding empathy with a godless world in that description of a life which is sinking in hopelessness. The search for an escape from the abyss is too evident to be denied. We do not need to invent sins or denounce evil ways of humanity. Unfolding history day by day illustrates in blinding flashes the darkness of the human soul. But the escape? We have abandoned the *deus ex machina* and may well have left the human race with the coldness of Jacques Monod's vision. There is struggle and there is ingenuity, there is increasing understanding of the human mind, but no true escape. The words of Freud are ominously true:

> Science can teach us how to avoid certain dangers and that there are some sufferings which it can successfully combat; it would be most unjust to deny that it is a powerful helper to men; but there are many situations in which it must leave a man his sufferings and can only advise him to submit to it.[28]

And Freud was not only concerned with physical suffering. The darkness of human life can be stoically endured, but that is not to give it meaning. To an extent, Viktor Frankl saw this in the development of his logotherapy as an extension of psychoanalysis. The logotherapist is not content to explain the situation to his patient and make him face up to it; he must give some sense of meaning in life. But in the end, a life is not justified by psychotherapy in any form. Freud understood this when he outlined the enormous appeal of religion. What Bonhoeffer talks about is not a religious doctrine – which can be an illusion, as Freud said – or, in Bonhoeffer's words, the 'vain repetition of articles of faith, a dead faith'.[29] Bonhoeffer talks of justification as an act of God, 'by grace alone'. And so did Luther.

There is no demythologising here. This is an experience which a Christian can testify to and then try to explain. This is not a matter of what you must believe before something can happen to you to lift you out of the abyss. It is the grace of God which unexpectedly comes to us. Those who sat in darkness have seen a great light! The word of God breaks in. All this takes place when Christ comes to men. Then the person who experiences the presence of Christ is no longer a lost life, but a justified life, justified by grace alone. But at once Bonhoeffer adds: 'Yet not only by grace alone, but also by faith alone . . . A life is not justified by love or by hope, but only by faith.'[30]

Believing in the presence of Christ sets life upon a new foundation, which is the life and death and resurrection of Jesus Christ by which we live. The alternative is ultimately to lose meaning in life. Words cannot completely explain this action of justifying or giving meaning to life. It is an act of God in grace which is not a convertible currency. Faith also is an action, but an action of a different kind. It is a submission to an action of God, and in this submission alone it is itself an action. There is thus a certainty about faith which has no comparison with the questioning and doubt of theological propositions. As Bonhoeffer says, 'Faith alone is certainty. Everything but faith is subject to doubt.'[31] It is the one access to the justification which is by grace alone, but in our lives accepted only by faith. But faith is never alone. Faith is the presence of Christ, and must therefore be accompanied by love and hope.

Bonhoeffer calls this event in a human life 'the last thing'. All else must be penultimate, with no value except in the light of the last word.

This word of the justifying grace of God must always be the ultimate word. We cannot think of our justification as something achieved, a result which might as well be at the beginning as at the end:

> The way from the penultimate to the ultimate can never be dispensed with. The word remains irreversibly the last; for otherwise it would be reduced to the quality of what is calculable, a merchandise, and would thereby be robbed of its divine character. Grace would be venal and cheap. It would not be a gift.[32]

The Christian way of life is thus related to this last word and finds meaning in it. In Christ the reality of God encounters the reality of the world and allows us to share in this meeting, so that the Christian life is a participation in the encounter of Christ with the world. That leaves open the whole of Christian ethics – the penultimate, which finds meaning in God's gracious act and which alone justifies us and can be received only by faith in the presence of Christ in our world – in life, in death and in resurrection. The word of God breaks in, and this is the meaning of it all; but there are stages on the way to the realisation of it in our own lives. The slave is not freed in order to become a Christian – the Christian slave is set free. The outcast is not given his rights, nor the hungry his bread, in order to become a Christian – the outcast Christian is given his rights, the hungry Christian his bread. This is fundamental to Bonhoeffer's way of thinking about the last thing:

> Only the triumphal entry of the Lord will bring with it the fulfilment of [humanity] and goodness. But a light is already shed by the coming Lord upon what is meant by being [human] and by being good in the way which is required for true preparation and expectation. It is only by reference to the Lord who is to come, and who has come, that we can know what it is to be [human] and to be good.[33]

7

RELIGIONLESS WORSHIP AND PRAYER

The crucial text for this chapter is the letter written to Eberhard Bethge on 30 April 1944.[1] There Bonhoeffer wrestled with the consequence of 'being radically without religion' for Christianity. He was missing friends like Bethge, with whom he could talk and try out his ideas. Now he was the lonely writer of letters, and consequently he leaves us with unanswered questions, but questions none the less which we cannot ignore. Always, what is central to his thinking is 'the question what Christianity really is, or indeed who Christ really is, for us today'.[2] He observes that you can no longer assume anything in the modern world. Words, whether theological or pious, will no longer answer the basic questions of humanity. The 'inner life' and 'conscience' are no longer adequate. In fact, it looks as though humanity is no longer 'religious'. Perhaps religion was only a stage in the human development. The consequence as he sees it is separation from the world, which means reducing Christianity to the few who are prepared to swallow it, or at least pretend to, and the 'unhappy people in their weaker moments'. If Christianity is for humanity in its fullness then we have to face the fact that religion has had its day. Then, the Western pattern of Christianity was a preliminary stage. What is Christianity today? Can Christ become the Lord of those who have no religion at all? 'If religion is only a garment of Christianity – and even this garment has looked very different at different times – then what is a religionless Christianity?'[3] In the midst of all this questioning, he asks: 'What is the place of worship [the cultus] and prayer in a religionless situation?'[4]

THE SIGNIFICANCE OF WORSHIP IN BONHOEFFER'S LIFE

All his life Dietrich Bonhoeffer had known the power of religion. As a young man in Rome he was overpowered by the liturgy of the Holy Week.[5] At Ettal, he felt completely at home with the religious life,[6] in fact he wrote some of his best theology there! When he was in prison, he kept to the church calendar and observed the feasts. The hymnbook and Bible were his sustenance. Perhaps most telling of all is the last religious service he conducted, a few days before he died.[7]

A group of them were being moved about as prisoners from one temporary prison after the other as the Allied armies advanced. In Schönberg, they were in a comparatively comfortable school. It was the Sunday after Easter, and it was suggested that they hold a service of worship. There were both Catholics and Protestants in the group, but that caused no difficulty. Confessional differences had become peripheral in the circumstances of their imprisonment. But there was one difficulty. Wassilev Kokorin, one of their number, the nephew of Molotov, was a convinced communist and therefore 'religionless'. Bonhoeffer judged the solidarity of their suffering more important than the sustenance of Christian fellowship in worship. He could not conduct a religious service which excluded one of their number. It was not possible until Kokorin himself had asked for the service – presumably, not because he believed in God, but because he believed in the group! As it turned out, the service itself was so powerful that other groups in the school wanted to smuggle Bonhoeffer over to them to conduct such a service. There was no time. Bonhoeffer was taken from them to his execution in Flossenburg.

The incident illustrates the importance of worship to Bonhoeffer, but also the readiness to accept a situation in which worship was denied because of whom it excluded.

THE 'ARCANE DISCIPLINE'

We have seen how Bonhoeffer called for a secular interpretation of biblical terms and how he illustrated the need for this in his 'baptismal sermon' for Dietrich Wilhelm Rüdiger Bethge. In that sermon, he looked forward to the time when the word would be spoken that liberated the world. But that was not yet. Meanwhile, he called for 'prayer and righteous action'.[8] He did not intend by this to convert the world, but to preserve the faith from violation by the world.

The letter to Bethge on 21 July 1944[9] expresses the same longing. In the loneliness of the day after the failure of the attempt on Hitler's life, Bonhoeffer wrote:

> These theological thoughts are, in fact, always occupying my mind; but there are times when I am just content to live the life of faith without worrying about its problems. At those times I simply take pleasure in the days' readings – in particular those of yesterday and today; and I'm always glad to go back to Paul Gerhardt's beautiful hymns.[10]

Bethge's judgement, which is confirmed by so many references in these prison letters, is that Bonhoeffer regarded an 'arcane discipline'[11] as an essential counterpoint of his non-religious interpretation. He does not resolve this counterpoint, but it is clear that he intends to preserve a 'genuine worship' and not impose it upon the world. He does not answer his question as to what is going to happen to the worship service.

It is, however, quite clear from the baptism sermon that Bonhoeffer had no view of doing away with the word, the sacrament and the community, replacing them by love. What he would not do was impose them upon the world. The 'mysteries' are to be kept sacred, preserved from violation by the world; but they are to be preserved in the church and the private devotions of the disciple. They are not to be used as powers to violate the autonomy of the world. Their relation to the world is found in the disciple's 'participation in the suffering of God in the secular life'.[12] This participation effects a new fusion of the disciple who is conformed to the likeness of the suffering of Christ. It is this which one day will make available the word of reconciliation and redemption. Then, as we have already quoted from the baptismal sermon, 'men will once more be called so to utter the word of God that the world will be changed and renewed by it. It will be a new language . . . [which will] shock people and yet overcome them by its power . . .'[13] Meanwhile, the mysteries are preserved by the arcane discipline. Prayer, worship, and 'assembling together' are essential – as food and drink to our bodily life. Those who are sustained by this discipline are called upon to interpret Christianity in a non-religious sense, but they cannot demonstrate or impose the nature of their sustenance. One day, perhaps, but not while the automatic relation of these mysteries and the world is broken. The great words of faith must not be jettisoned, but continue to live in the arcane discipline.

There is a preserving and a waiting in Bonhoeffer's thought. Again, in the baptismal sermon, he points out the perilous and yet welcome state in which his generation finds itself:

'We shall have to keep our lives rather than shape them, to endure rather than forge ahead. But we do want to preserve a heritage for you, the rising generation, so that you will have the resources for building a new and better life'.[14]

WORSHIP IN THE YEARS THAT FOLLOWED

That was more than forty years ago. The generation which Bonhoeffer saw as 'the rising generation', for whom something was preserved, is now middle-aged! The churches have desperately tried to reform the style of their worship in order to halt the decline. Bonhoeffer warned about this:

'We are not yet out of the melting pot, and every attempt to hasten matters will only delay the Church's conversion and purgation.'[15]

But how long are we to wait?

There is a group within the Church of England (and of course other churches too) who resist changes in the traditional forms of worship. They protested when The Alternative Service Book was issued in 1980. They resisted the use of modern translations of the Bible in worship. Some of the protest was mere obscurantism. But Bonhoeffer indicates to us that there may be deeper reasons, even if they are not always too well expressed. In times such as ours, when the majority of people are strangers to worship, the attempts to adapt worship forms to attract non-worshippers may lead to the loss of true worship. There is a danger that the worship of the church may be profaned by the world, communicated before its time. The case for such protest in the Church of England was put very clearly by John Gummer, a Member of Parliament who is a devout worshipper in the Church of England and a member of Synod. It was in a TV interview in which he attacked the Bishop of Durham for calling certain fundamental doctrines in question and the Alternative Service Book for dividing the Church. He pointed out that the Church of England had survived and retained within it a wide variety of people who had different theological views by insisting upon a limited number of fundamentals. Among these was the Book of Common Prayer. High and Low Churchmen could kneel together at the Communion Rail at any Anglican Church with perfect harmony, despite differences in attitudes to the hierarchy or biblical interpretations.

There is a similar example in the Roman Catholic Church. The decisions of the Second Vatican Council which insisted upon the celebration of the mass in the vernacular led to a deep sense of loss by many who had felt the mystery of the mass being profaned and divided by splitting into different languages.

The question is thus posed whether the mysteries should be preserved or communicated. If the former, then a monastic existence is maintained by the church, although its members go forth from the monastery to perform their work strengthened. Their only Christian communication is the quality of their lives. No effort is made to bring people into church for worship which they clearly would not understand. Meanwhile, the children of believers are taught in home and church to enter into the mysteries. This begins to look more and more like a mystery religion or even a secret society. Yet, in effect, it is not too far removed from what is common practice in many parishes. It can be attractive even to the doubters. The philosopher C. E. M. Joad was converted to Christianity, not by an evangelist or even by argument, but by the faithful performance of the mysteries in the local village churches which he visited. This has also been the strength of the Orthodox churches, and has preserved them through centuries of alien rule and persecution.

The alternative is to attempt to communicate. This too is well illustrated in the years since Bonhoeffer. The massive Billy Graham rallies have presented a highly attractive, charismatic character, supported by music of good entertainment-value. They have brought huge crowds of people together and persuaded many that they are the people to whom you should belong if you want to be happy, now and through all eternity. The Christian gospel is, 'Get right with God.' A method of persuasion has been worked out and it is effective. Many would never have considered joining with the worshippers of the Lord Jesus Christ if they had not been attracted to a Billy Graham rally or some such mass meeting. The same can happen at the local level. A church may consider its services too formal and make changes to attract outsiders, principally young people, because church attendance is often confined to the middle class and the older generation.

Over the whole range of liturgical experience, from the Catholic tradition to the Free Churches, there has been a recognition that the liturgy of the church is another world. What is to be done? If young people are at home in *their* music, hymns must be written to relate to it. If young people are speaking a special kind of language which is rarely if ever used in church, the church must learn how to integrate that language into worship. If young people relate to one another in easy, informal gestures, while in church the movements are formalised, then should the gestures not be incorporated within the liturgy?

All this has been done. New hymnbooks have incorporated different kinds of music and folk masses have become popular, with such composers as Geoffrey Beaumont pioneering the way. The Alternative Service Book has modernised the language of prayer and responses. What J. B. Phillips refused to do with the Collects, when asked to do for them what he had done for the New Testament, has now been done for them in the ASB. A simple example of changing the important language of responses is in the congregational response to the priest's 'The Lord be with you.' The traditional answer, which still carries an aura for older people, 'And with thy spirit,' has become the banal 'And also with you.' Efforts have also been made to modernise the Lord's Prayer, but these have not been generally accepted.

All this is a little like tinkering if Bonhoeffer is right in his assessment that a generation without religion no longer worships, 'not even idols'. His conclusions are reinforced by the fact that despite all the changes, the general pattern of church attendance has declined. There are local exceptions, but it is impossible to escape the obvious fact that worship is becoming a minority activity, and that minority is getting smaller and older.

THE CHARISMATIC MOVEMENT

The rewriting of our prayers and the new settings to our hymns, the informal giving of the peace and the efforts to make the fellowship more warm, will go on. But the real changes in worship seem to have come mostly in the new experience of the Holy Spirit. This is usually accompanied by a new sense of hope, not as a tranquilliser, but as an essential ingredient of the Christian faith.

In 1974, Cardinal Suenens published his assessment of what was happening in *Une Nouvelle Pentecôte?*, translated a year later and published by Darton, Longman and Todd as *A New Pentecost?* In that book he shows that the Second Vatican Council was a turning-point in the history of the Roman Catholic Church. It was called by Pope John XXIII because he recognised that the new world was changing around the church. He wanted renewal and unity and the Second Vatican Council, aided by such men as Henri de Lubac and Cardinal

Suenens himself, carried through by Pope Paul VI, quickened the church. It overhauled its cumbersome apparatus and set itself on course for the twentieth century.

The most obvious effects were changes in worship and in relations with other churches. But the renewal went much deeper than was at first apparent. Without knowing it, Pope John had recognised the need to give birth to a new expression of the church's faith and practice. It was the Ecumenical Patriarch, however, who most clearly saw this, although far less change took place in his own church. Suenens quotes the Patriarch Athenagoras:

> The world today is giving birth, and birth is always accompanied by hope. We view this present situation with a great Christian hope and a deep sense of our responsibility for the kind of world that will be born of this travail. This is the hour of the Church: united, it must offer to this world being born, some Christian orientations as its future.[16]

That was in January 1969. It was a time of great confusion. A little later, Cardinal Suenens was asked by the editor of *The Critic* why he was a man of hope, and he replied, 'Because I believe in the Holy Spirit.' That answer carried with it his support of the charismatic movement in the Roman Catholic Church. He expanded on his brief comment at the request of the editor, and it was published on the front page of his publication at the end of 1970, then used later by the Cardinal for his Pentecost message in 1974:

Why are You a Man of Hope?
Because I believe that God is born anew each morning,
because I believe he is creating the world at this very
      moment. He did not create it at a distant and
      long-forgotten moment in time.
It is happening now: we must therefore be ready to expect
      the unexpected from God.
The ways of Providence are by nature surprising.
We are not prisoners of determinism nor of the sombre
      prognostications of sociologists.
God is here, near us, unforeseeable and loving.

I am a man of hope, not for human reasons nor from any
    natural optimism.
But because I believe the Holy Spirit is at work in the
    Church and in the world, even when his name remains
    unheard.
I am an optimist because I believe the Holy Spirit is the
    Spirit of creation.
To those who welcome him he gives each day fresh liberty
    and renewed joy and trust.
The long history of the Church is filled with the wonders
    of the Holy Spirit.
Think only of the prophets and saints who, in times of
    darkness, have discovered a spring of grace and shed
    beams of light on our path.
I believe in the surprises of the Holy Spirit.
John XXIII came as a surprise, and the Council, too.
They were the last things we expected.
Who would dare to say that the love and imagination of
    God were exhausted?
To hope is a duty, not a luxury.
To hope is not to dream, but to turn dreams into reality.
Happy are those who dream dreams and are ready to pay
    the price to make them come true.[17]

That is the charter of the charismatic movement at its best.
Of course, there are many counterfeits, which take hold only
of the froth and excitement, the sensational gifts and un-
restrained worship, which often divide the church and forget
our Lord's prayer for unity.

The authentic charismatic movement which has come as a
gift of the Spirit to a tired church blows like the wind and
teaches us to worship God in new forms. These new forms,
which Bonhoeffer foresaw would one day come, are not
fashioned by human reason or products of a desire to communicate to a new generation. They preserve the mysteries
and do not profane them. They do not impose a structure of
doctrine upon the world, they liberate men and women to
worship God without fear. They carry joy and hope into the
very presence of God.

Apart from this sense of joy and hope, there are three
outward manifestations: speaking with tongues, healing and
mystical communion with God. None of these things is new,
but they have been repressed in the church for so long that the
wind of the Spirit needed to blow through our imprisoned
worship to liberate them again.

Speaking with Tongues

As early as Paul's first letter to the Corinthians, the dangers
of this manifestation of the Spirit were recognised. It is
impressive and gives a lift to worship when it is genuine. It
cannot be planned, and it challenges the orderliness of our
worship. There is no place for it in Matins and the equally
rigid Free Church hymn-sandwich is also confused when it
appears. A person – and usually the most unlikely person – is
taken possession of by the Holy Spirit and speaks a language
which he (or more often she) does not understand. It is a
message, usually of encouragement or uplift, which as Paul
insists, should be interpreted by another member of the
congregation who is moved to declare in the vernacular what
the Spirit is saying to the church. 'He who has an ear, let him
hear what the Spirit says to the churches'.

Paul points out that there should be no boasting or sense of
superiority on the part of the one (or two, if we include the
interpreter) who is used merely as a channel of the Spirit. He
also insists that the gift of tongues is not an isolated gift. There
are others of equal importance. Tongue speaking heads none
of his lists. To Corinth he writes: 'And God has appointed in
the church first apostles, second prophets, third teachers,
then workers of miracles, then healers, helpers, administra-
tors, speakers in various kinds of tongues' (1 Corinthians
12:28). He proceeds to challenge the idea that any Christian
should possess all these gifts. Each to his gift, but the church
possesses all. Then in a curious admonition, he says, 'But
earnestly desire the higher gifts' (1 Corinthians 12:31). What
are these? The famous 1 Corinthians 13 follows, with its
overwhelming claim for love. In fact no spiritual gift is worth
anything which is not set in love. For Jesus gave us but one

commandment, '. . . love one another as I have loved you' (John 15:12). All spiritual gifts find their place in charismatic worship, but the presence of the Holy Spirit in such gatherings is tested not by tongues, nor by miraculous healings, nor by great preaching, nor by apostolic authority, nor by correct doctrine, important as all of these are. The presence of the Holy Spirit with the manifold gifts of the Spirit is marked by the love we have for one another. Without it, the worship itself is rendered void.

On the Day of Pentecost, 'they were all together in one place'. The love which marked the earliest community of believers made it possible for the Spirit to quicken the tongues of those who were assembled so that they 'began to speak in other tongues, as the Spirit gave them utterance' (Acts 2.1–4). That was followed by all the other gifts – preaching, prophecy, healing, *etc.* The only preparation that we can make for this tongue speaking is to learn to love one another. That will mean that when 'one member suffers, all suffer together', and 'if one member is honoured, all rejoice together' (1 Corinthians 12:26).

Cardinal Suenens, in a very enlightening section of the book already quoted, attempts to describe the role of speaking in tongues in worship:

> A newcomer to a prayer meeting is often intrigued to hear from time to time, one person – or the whole group – beginning to pray or sing in tongues. His first impression is one of uneasiness prompted by this spontaneous verbal expression, in which syllables succeed one another, forming phrases that are unintelligible. It is important to understand 'glossolalia', neither minimizing nor exaggerating the importance of this mode of prayer. It is not a miracle, it is not pathological.[18]

Those who have genuinely experienced this mode of prayer confess that it brings a freedom from inhibitions which have previously blocked their way to God and their relationship with others. It is in fact a liberating experience. If a person once allows himself or herself to let go, and then behaves in a way that appears foolish, there is an act of humility which leads to the joy of praying in a way that surpasses the use of words and human reasoning. It also brings peace and openness to others for spiritual communication.

Speaking in tongues does not rule out other forms of prayer, but rather enhances these other forms, giving them life where they have become routine. Paul is very careful to avoid too much attention being given to this 'gift'.[19] It is not for all, and it is the least of all spiritual gifts. But those who have experienced it in its authentic, Christian form, find that it is a way into other gifts. Cardinal Suenens compares it to a little door into the great halls of spirituality.[20] It is a grace, but a humble grace, which has to do with love, which again in Paul's words is 'patient and kind . . . not jealous or boastful . . . not arrogant or rude . . . not insisting on its own way . . . not irritable or resentful . . . not [rejoicing] at wrong, but rejoicing in the right . . . bearing all things, believing all things, hoping all things, enduring all things' (1 Corinthians 13:4–6). Those are the tests to apply to discern the spirit of 'tongue speaking', whether it be of God. If it fails that test, it is without love and is therefore 'a noisy gong or a clanging cymbal' (1 Corinthians 13:1). But immersed in love and answering to the test, it is a part of the liberation of worship which Bonhoeffer looked for. Its revival in our day across the board of Christian traditions is surely part of God's healing.

Healing

Another gift of the Spirit in worship which has been revived in our day is the gift of healing. So much has been written on this revival of the 'forgotten talent' that we need not repeat it all here. What concerns us is the proper place of healing in relation to our worship and prayer. We pray for the sick, but we tend to assume that all we are doing is asking God to support doctors and surgeons and help the patient to endure the pain and frustration which he or she must expect as part of the slow process of healing. Theoretically, we all say and believe that only God can heal. An alternative statement to that in our religionless world is, 'the body must do its own healing'. The doctors and surgeons who understand the working of the body are best equipped to prepare the shattered parts that they might grow together. Where does prayer come into all that? Many diverse experiences have shown that healing can be aided by a loving environment, a sensitive touch, an atmosphere of prayer. This is explained by saying that disease is more than physical. The psychotherapist sets the mind free to receive its healing, and that in turn allows the body to heal itself.

But the word mind is much wider than all the wisdom of psychology can explain. There is a spiritual health and a spiritual disease, and these are interconnected with the mental and the physical. The trilogy of body, mind and spirit still has some meaning, provided we recognise that they are all part of the same complex. Many healing movements have illustrated the effectiveness of this way of thinking. But our question is, What part does healing have in the worship of the church? It is impossible to ignore the fact that healing played a large part in the ministry of Jesus, and that frequently this occurred in a synagogue. Peter and John approached worship in the temple, and on the way healed a crippled man 'in the name of Jesus Christ of Nazareth' (Acts 3:6). The instructions given in the Epistle of James, which presumably reflect the practice of the early church, are quite clear:

> Is any among you sick? Let him call for the elders of the church, and let them pray over him, anointing him with oil in the name of the Lord; and the prayer of faith will save the sick man, and the Lord will raise him up; and if he has committed sins, he will be forgiven. Therefore confess your sins to one another, and pray for one another, that you may be healed. (James 5:14–16)

There is a confidence in the power of prayer to heal, but healing is never merely physical healing. It is wrapped up in forgiveness.

I am always grateful that the synoptic evangelists recorded a failed attempt at healing by the disciples (Matthew 17:14–21, and parallels). There is no guaranteed method by which the church can heal, but healing belongs in its worship. The charismatic movement, including the earlier Pentecostal sects, have taught us that healing belongs in our worship. Many attempts have been made to recover it. Some have been counterfeit. They have been sensational, sometimes intending to bring fame to the healer or to attract more people into the church. The true test of healing is whether the person healed is nourished within a loving community, and the person who is not healed is treated with the same love and care.

It is possible to see worship as part of the healing process. When it is, then it must always be inclusive of forgiveness. At Burrswood in Surrey, there is a house which resembles a nursing home. There medical expertise and counselling are available, but prayer is also made, and at healing services those who thank God for what he has done through doctors and surgeons find healing in worship. At the Parish Church of St Marylebone in London, the crypt which once housed the dead now has consulting rooms and offices with holistic medicine, a general practitioner of the National Health Service, counselling and befriending facilities, dance therapy and the Churches' Council for Health and Healing. The church is working side by side with the healing professions; and above, in the magnificent church itself, the Anglican liturgy is worthily performed with music of a particularly high standard. Part of that liturgy is a Healing Service once a month. There is nothing sensational about such a service, but those who in their sickness call for the help of the church are able to come forward and feel the healing power of the Holy Spirit ministered through the celebrant as he lays his hands on them. The gift of healing is recovered in the worship of the Church of St Marylebone.

Mystical Communion

When he returned from England to set up the seminary for students in the Confessing Church, first at Zingst and then Finkenwalde, Bonhoeffer abandoned his plan to visit Gandhi in India. But he did visit three Anglican communities – Mirfield, Kelham and the Cowley Fathers at Oxford – during his time in England. He was impressed by an element in worship which was lacking in his German Protestantism. It might be defined as 'meditation', and he was particularly impressed by the intensity of prayer based upon Psalm 119.[21] He introduced something of this into Finkenwalde. One form was to read the Bible passage without commentary and for a prolonged period to think upon it, reading it again and again until it began to speak to the student. The students had been used to working at the meaning of the passage and discussing it. A new dimension came into their 'religion' with this exercise. Bonhoeffer felt the same attraction at Ettal.

From time to time in the history of the church 'mystics' have arisen who are a problem to systematic theologians. They do not study doctrine, but depend upon a direct communion, a 'mystical communion' with God. This develops a spirituality which enlarges the liturgy and biblical studies into a new space. The Christian development of 'meditation' associated by Geoffrey Harding with 'relaxation exercises' has attracted interest from the secular community. At St Mary, Woolnoth, Geoffrey Harding started relaxation and meditation classes which became popular with the business community of the City. This has continued since his death and has been repeated in many other places. The business community, of course, did not see this as a mystical communion with God, but they were on the edge of something which is gradually affecting the worship of the churches. Meditation groups are part of this development, where the essence of communion with God is not argued about or even learnt, it is experienced. Some of the great words which Bonhoeffer talked about in the baptismal sermon, as words we hardly dare to use because we understand them as little as an infant being baptised, are not being explained in these groups, but spoken – and they are liberating, as Bonhoeffer suggests.

Another example of a recovered sense of mystical communion comes within the experience of black churches. Many of these are Pentecostal, whatever name they give themselves. They have healing and speaking with tongues. But there is also ecstatic dancing and trance-like awareness of the spirit of God. In other churches with charismatic tendencies we are seeing the beginning of new gestures and experiences. The clapping of hands during hymns, dancing in the service, various ways of giving the 'kiss of peace', repetitive lines in hymns *etc.* give a warmth and feeling of surrender to a community. Although this may be feared as 'getting out of hand', it is often experienced as a closeness to God which words alone cannot achieve.

We may add to this the growth of literature on spirituality and the seeking of an experience of God in the closeness of human fellowship.

The Focolare Movement

At the time Bonhoeffer was in prison, a young Italian woman reacted to the bombing of her native town of Trento in Northern Italy by reading the sayings of Jesus and gathering around her a group of young women. She formed these women into a family. They had all lost much, and sought an ideal which could not be destroyed. They found the ideal in God, and tried to live the verses of the gospel day by day. Chiara Lubich, who formed this group, later to become an international and ecumenical movement of great significance, developed a spirituality which came out of her experience of God, her deep sense of commitment, her love for others, her Catholic worship and her discovery of what Jesus said in the gospels. I have told the full story of her experience in my book *Chiara*,[22] and of the ongoing Focolare Movement under a further figure of charismatic influence, Igino Giordani, in a second book, *The Fire of Love*.[23] Both Chiara Lubich and Igino Giordani are examples of those who have had mystical communion with God. And there have been other communities based upon an increasing degree of personal experience of this kind. The Focolare Movement shows clearly how such mystical communion can be integrated into the worship of the local church.

THE WAY FORWARD IN WORSHIP

Bonhoeffer faced the problems of worship in a religionless world. He rejected the elitism which reserved worship only

for the spiritually minded or mentally limited. Yet he wished
to preserve the mysteries. Theology of worship and the
experience of new dimensions in worship have pointed the
way ahead. Much has changed since his day. He would have
found it difficult to approve of some of the changes, and I
fancy that his tidy German mind would have found the
charismatic movement 'hard to bear'. But he saw already the
value of worship in the black churches in America when he
was a Sloane Fellow at Union Theological Seminary in his
twenties. He compared such worship favourably with the
traditional worship of the fashionable Riverside Church
nearby. Later, when he wrote of America after his second and
last visit in 1939, he was again enthusiastic about the
contribution of what he calls 'the negro churches' to our
understanding of worship. He lists the 'negro spirituals' as
one of the contributions. But, as though anticipating his later
thinking on a society without religion, he adds:

> The turning aside of the newly arising generation of Negroes
> from the faith of their elders, which, with its strong eschatological
> orientation, seems to them to be a hindrance to the progress of
> their race and their rights, is one of the ominous signs of a failing
> of the church in past centuries and a hard problem for the future.
> If it has come about that today the 'black Christ' has to be led into
> the field against the 'white Christ' by a young Negro poet, then a
> deep cleft in the church of Jesus Christ is indicated.[24]

Our failure in Britain to include the black Christians in our
churches, leaving them mainly to form their own, raises a
similar question for us. It could be that their failure to find
satisfaction in our white churches was not racial, nor entirely
cultural, but due to the failure of our worship. Many of the
signs of life which have been indicated in this chapter are
living elements of black worship. We have perhaps to learn
from the black churches, not so much our theology or our
liturgy, but how to worship with our whole being and 'so to
utter the word of God that the world will be changed and
renewed by it'.[25]
    That will begin in our worship.

8

WHAT DO WE REALLY BELIEVE?

The pilgrim church has carried through the centuries the massive accumulating luggage of 'Christian doctrine'. The weight of it has suffocated its spontaneity; the need to protect it has made it security-conscious and has led to interconfessional disputes of hideous proportions. Artists and sensitive souls who have loved the church have constantly tried to recapture that lost spontaneity. They have usually been denounced by the 'defenders of the faith', concerned more with defending the church than communicating the liberty it offers through Christ.

Sister Estelle, in her lively hymn comparing the church with the Hebrew slaves led out of Egypt by Moses, puts it clearly into her second verse:

> 'Don't get too set in your ways',
> The Lord said,
> 'Each step is only a phase'
> The Lord said,
> 'I'll go before you and I shall be a sign
> To guide my travelling wandering race,
> You're the people of God.'[1]

And the chorus emphasises 'the travelling, wandering race' who are the people of God. Many different traditions within the church are singing that hymn with evident enthusiasm.

The tune which Sister Estelle has composed for the words assures you that either you get carried along with it or you do not sing it. The instructions for singing are, 'Bounce this off the tongue.' And yet each tradition has gathered through the centuries so much baggage and so many set ideas and so much prejudice and such a defensive attitude, that it is hard to see any of them as a 'travelling, wandering race'. Instead of pitching tents at night, we have all built rickety palaces, and we know how prone they are to collapse before critical winds! And there have not been lacking such winds from the most penetrating minds.

The poets have raised their voices often in protest against the church, or more often against the priests, who imprison Christ and withhold the liberation which he offers. None more clearly than Byron in his 'The Prayer of Nature':

Father of Light! great God of Heaven!
Hear'st thou the accents of despair?
Can guilt like man's be e'er forgiven?
Can vice atone for crimes by prayer?

Father of Light on thee I call!
Thou seest my soul is dark within;
Thou who canst mark the sparrow's fall,
Avert from me the death of sin.

No shrine I seek, no sects unknown;
Oh, point to me the path of truth!
Thy dread omnipotence I own;
Spare, yet amend, the faults of youth.

– Let bigots rear a gloomy fane,
Let superstition hale the pile,
Let priests, to spread their sable reign,
With tales of mystic rites beguile.

Shall man confine his Maker's sway
To Gothic domes of mouldering stone?
The temple is the face of day;
Earth, ocean, heaven, thy boundless throne.

Shall man condemn his race to hell,
Unless they bend in pompous form?
Tell us that all, for one who fell,
Must perish in the mingling storm?

> Shall each pretend to reach the skies,
> Yet doom his brother to expire,
> Whose soul a different hope supplies,
> Or doctrine less severe inspire?
>
> Shall these by creeds they can't expound,
> Prepare a fancied bliss or woe?
> Shall reptiles, grovelling on the ground,
> Their great Creator's purpose know?
>
> Shall those who live for self alone,
> Whose years float on in daily crime –
> Shall they by Faith for guilt atone,
> And live beyond the bounds of Time?[2]

There is more, and there are other poets, and have been through the centuries. Even the gentle W. H. Auden, in his 'Christmas Oratorio', can imply the need for questioning and searching to find who Christ is for us today. Two lines link his questing soul to the search of one of the wise men:

> To discover how to be truthful *now*
> Is the reason I follow this star.

John Robinson, who quotes those two lines in his book *The Difference in Being a Christian Today*, comments with the help of Kierkegaard, that Pilate's question, 'What is truth?', becomes for the Christian, 'What is my relation to the truth, what is true for me?'[3]

That unpacks the luggage of the centuries, so that to be a Christian is not to accept what tradition has taught that you must believe, but to be committed to Jesus Christ and to have the courage to face and answer the question, '*What do I really believe?*'

TELLING THE TRUTH

Towards the end of 1943, twice in his letters to Bethge, Bonhoeffer refers to an essay he has written in Tegel on 'Speaking the Truth'.[4] This essay, now called 'What is Meant by "Telling the Truth"?' has been printed at the end of his *Ethics*.[5] In it he distinguishes different ways of speaking the truth, according to the person addressed and the situation. Speaking the truth to a parent is different from speaking the truth to a wife or husband, to a stranger or to one from whom you have been estranged: 'It is only the cynic who claims "to speak the truth" at all times and in all places to all men in the same way, but who, in fact, displays nothing but a lifeless image of the truth.'[6] Such a one who claims that he must tell the truth regardless of human weakness destroys the living truth between persons. He wounds shame, desecrates mystery, breaks confidence, betrays the community in which he lives, and laughs arrogantly at the devastation he has wrought. And Bonhoeffer adds, 'There is a truth which is of Satan.'[7]

He then tackles the concept of 'a living truth', which has its dangers, because it comes under the suspicion of being adaptable – to suit specific occasions. He gives an interesting example[8] of a teacher who has asked a question which it is not proper for the teacher to ask. The teacher asks the child in front of his class if it is true that his father often comes home drunk. Although it is true, and the child knows it is true, he denies it. Bonhoeffer justifies his answer. The teacher's question has put the child in a situation for which he is not yet prepared. He senses an unjustified interference in the order of the family, which he must oppose. The child ought now to find a way of responding which would comply both with the order of the school and the order of the family. He lacks experience and is unable to respond in the correct way to satisfy both institutions. His simple 'No' is untrue; but he has to find a way of saying that the family has an integrity of its own and the teacher has no right to interfere with it. In this way, Bonhoeffer shows that a lie is far more than 'a conscious discrepancy between thought and speech'.[9] He works out conditions under which we may speak the truth:

1. By perceiving who causes me to speak and what entitles me to speak.
2. By perceiving the place at which I stand.

3. By relating to this context the object about which I am making some assertion.[10]

In the letters which Bethge received with reference to this essay, Bonhoeffer points out that there is a proper place for concealment.[11] The essay was unfinished, but these three points are sufficiently commented upon to help us see how Bonhoeffer considers we should communicate our own Christian faith.

We speak of it because we wish to share that faith with others; we are entitled to speak of it because we have experienced its effect upon our own lives; and we choose the appropriate time and place when and where we speak. Then we must relate our faith to the context; that is, saying as much and concealing as much as we deem appropriate.

The importance of Bonhoeffer's essay on telling the truth is very considerable for the witness of the church. But behind it lies the sensitivity and the sincerity of the faith which is believed. To ourselves, we must face the question, 'What do I really believe?'

One immediate reference is to the repeating of the creed which I personally may not believe, or at least have serious doubts about: 'conceived of the Holy Ghost, born of the Virgin Mary', 'the resurrection of the body', 'descended into hell', *etc.* Karl Barth calls upon us to 'entrench ourselves persistently behind the "faith of the church"'.[12] But this is to avoid the honest question. It may however be appropriate to repeat a creed in church if we keep to the plural 'We believe . . .', because in that context we are prepared to stand with the church in solidarity. But that occasion when we are speaking on behalf of the church, with the church, does not allow us to make that creed a condition for being a Christian. It may be appropriate to conceal our doubts in a public service of worship, but it is not appropriate to say to another person, 'This you must believe . . .'

At the end of Bonhoeffer's *Ethics*, where Bethge has put this essay, he points out that it was unfinished, but quotes some comments by Bonhoeffer from a letter dated 5 December 1943 (Advent 2).[13] The end of that quote will help to clarify this paragraph:

'Speaking the truth' . . . means, in my opinion, saying how something really is – that is, showing respect for secrecy, intimacy, and concealment. 'Betrayal', for example, is not truth, any more than are flippancy, cynicism, etc. What is secret may be revealed only in confession, i.e. in the presence of God.[14]

RADICAL CHRISTIANITY

Bonhoeffer's *Letters and Papers from Prison* was first published in Britain by the SCM Press in 1953. It was immediately noted by theologians and broadcasters. The Third Programme of the BBC put out many discussions which led to comments and disputes in Oxford and Cambridge. But its impact was not widely felt. When it appeared as a Collins Fontana paperback in 1959, it made more impact, but the man who sent it speeding through the land was John Robinson, then Bishop of Woolwich.

After a particularly busy year, Robinson spent Christmas 1961 in bed with a painful back. While recovering from this, lying flat on his back and unable to read, his wife Ruth read to him a collection of sermons by Paul Tillich, *The Shaking of the Foundations*.[15] It spoke to his problems with the secular city to which he was trying to minister.

About that time, others were recognising the changing face of Britain and the isolation of the Church of England. In America, Gibson Winter had brought out *The Suburban Captivity of the Churches*,[16] showing the limited appeal of the church to the mass of the population. The church had become a class church. Many in England and Scotland were pointing out the failure of the church to reach the 'working class'. And after a survey of the church and people in Sheffield, Ted Wickham had coined the sentence in the context of industrial England: 'The church has not lost the industrial workers; it never had them.' Others were joking at the continuing title of the principal priest of the Church of England in urban Manchester: 'The Rural Dean of Manchester'. Again in America, Harvey Cox, in *The Secular City*,[17] had described urban life as divorced from the thinking and ethics of the church or Christianity – possibly even from religion as such.

John Robinson's own experience in Southwark, which was so different from his earlier time in Bristol, and even more different from his days in Cambridge, made him alter his view that the decline of the churches was about to change. He was already well acquainted with the radical writing of Rudolf Bultmann, which showed the need for 'demythologising' the stories of the New Testament before they could be significant for a culture without myths. He also read Bonhoeffer's *Letters and Papers from Prison*, and all this writing seemed to form into a pattern around his own experiences. He consulted with friends and fellow theologians and sent a copy of his draft manuscript to John Wren-Lewis, 'a young industrial scientist [at ICI] and lay theologian whose pungent criticisms of the contemporary religious scene in articles and [Third Programme] broadcasts had attracted [Robinson's] attention'.[18] John Wren-Lewis was a powerful influence on John Robinson because he was prepared to ask what Christians really believed and how what they believed fitted in to the way they ran their daily life. He saw secularism not as an enemy, but as the element within which Christianity has to live. He saw little sign that the church had recognised this. It was like a fish fighting against having to live in water.

Robinson's *Honest to God* was published in March 1963 and made an immediate impact. It was dependent upon many sources and many very English experiences, but it raised the basic Bonhoeffer question, 'What do we really believe?' Within six months there were nine impressions of the book and it made a fortune for the SCM Press, which under the leadership of David Edwards had received the manuscript and seized upon the title with enthusiasm from the start.

In the 'eye of the storm', Robinson broadcast a talk on the Third Programme with the title, 'On Being a Radical'.[19] In this talk, he distinguished the radical from the revolutionary and the reformist. The reformist tinkers with the machinery of orthodoxy to enable it to continue as before. The revolutionary insists that the whole structure must be changed if man is ever to be free. The radical, however,

must be a man of roots . . . And that is partly why in our rootless world there are so few genuine radicals . . .

The roots of the radical, moreover, must go deep enough to provide the security from which to question, even to the fundamentals. No one can be a radical who is uncertain of his tenure – intellectually, morally, or culturally. Only the man who knows he cannot lose what the Sabbath stands for can afford to criticize it radically. Faith alone can dare to doubt – to the depths.[20]

John Robinson caught the mood of many, particularly in the Church of England at that time, although he and his supporters were attacked violently by those who did not want to disturb the established situation which had served England well for four centuries or more, with only the occasional refurbishing.

Alec Vidler was one of those on whom Robinson could count. Vidler's symposium *Soundings*, published in 1962,[21] brought together a company of healthy radicals who were committed and whose faith was strong enough to ask radical questions. Vidler had welcomed anything that kept the frontiers of the church open to the world and deplored all that turned it in upon itself as a 'religious organization or episcopalian sect'. Like John Robinson, he was not proposing a new model for the church, but being honest and facing up to the 'obstinate questionings' which speak for the need of a 'reluctant revolution'. I suspect Vidler was less reluctant than John Robinson.[22]

Much earlier, Herbert Butterfield, in his *Christianity and History* (1949) had given a few lines at the end of that book which were among the most quoted at the time:

There are times when we can never meet the future with sufficient elasticity of mind, especially if we are locked in the contemporary systems of thought. We can do worse than remember a principle which both gives us a firm Rock and leaves us the maximum elasticity for our minds: the principle; Hold to Chirst and for the rest be totally uncommitted.[23]

Another memorable book of these early 1960s was Harry Williams' *The True Wilderness*. In 1965, the preface to that book spoke the word of total honesty which we were later very much to associate with this writer: 'I resolved that I would not preach about any aspect of Christian belief unless it had become part of my own life-blood.'[24]

In similar vein, Bonhoeffer in his 'Outline for a Book', complaining that Karl Barth and the Confessing Church had by hiding behind the 'faith of the church' evaded the honest question as to what we really believe, could say: 'That is why the air is not quite fresh, even in the Confessing Church.'[25]

DENOMINATIONAL DISPUTES

Bonhoeffer was a convinced Lutheran and a teacher of Lutheran theology. As a young man studying in New York, he found the freewheeling theology of America most distasteful. He believed in a good – and serious – theological framework for a Christian life. To the very end he was convinced of this. Writing to Rössler from New York on 11 December 1930, he complains:

> I have seldom found it so hard to accept Christmas in the right way . . . my hope to find Heb. 12.1 ['Therefore since we are surrounded by so great a cloud of witnesses, let us also lay aside every weight . . .'] fulfilled here has been bitterly disappointed. Besides, they find German theology so utterly local, they simply don't understand it here: they laugh at Luther.[26]

Meanwhile, his friends back in Germany were resisting national socialism, which many churches were making into the new religion – or as Rössler calls it, 'the new paganism'. They discovered that its unmasking and attacking was much more difficult than the old battles with free-thinking religion, 'because it goes around in Christian clothing'. And Bonhoeffer would most certainly have agreed. He did not want a new liberal theology which ironed out all the differences. His support for the ecumenical movement was not because he wanted a compromise between the theologies of the different denominations, but because he wanted a common search for the truth.

In the 'Outline for a Book' Bonhoeffer talks of antiquated controversies which may at any time be revived with passion. And while these no longer carry conviction, he is not advocating a theology-less church. He has convictions, pared down no doubt at the end, but firmly held. The denominational disputes may no longer be valid, but 'the faith of the Bible and Christianity' stands and is, in fact, not dependent on these issues.

He later grew to recognise a form of secularism as maturity, but in his student days in New York he saw the danger of secularising Christianity. That danger lay in an inadequate theology:

> The theological atmosphere of Union Theological Seminary is accelerating the process of the secularisation of Christianity in America. Its criticism is directed essentially against the fundamentalists and to a certain extent also against the radical humanists in Chicago; it is healthy and necessary. But there is no sound basis on which one can rebuild after demolition. It is carried away with the general collapse. A seminary in which it can come about that a large number of students laugh out loud in a public lecture at the quoting of a passage from Luther's *De servo arbitrio* on sin and forgiveness because it seems to them to be comic has evidently completely forgotten what Christian theology by its very nature stands for.[27]

Like any German theologian, Bonhoeffer was rightly proud of the magnificent structure of university theology among the Protestants of Germany. But when the crisis came in 1933, the German Christians, who had supported a National Socialist Movement, were unable to avoid theological discussion. The church struggle with the Confessing Church was not over politics or even church politics, but over theology and faith. These determined the real controversies of the Protestant church in the Third Reich. Bonhoeffer distinguished between this necessary theological battle and the outworn disputes which now fell away in the face of more serious opposition.

THE BETHEL CONFESSION

Although the famous Barmen Declaration was ultimately adopted by the Confessing Church, Bonhoeffer had little to do with its final form. In fact, he had worked (primarily with

Hermann Sasse) under the fatherly supervision of Friedrich von Bodelschwingh, in 1933 at 'Bethel'. 'Bethel' was Von Bodelschwingh's 'City of Hope', developed around an Epileptic Institution.

The Confessing Church had fought church elections and cared for deprived pastors through the Pastors' Emergency League. In August they started an extensive programme of practical community work and church theological discussions. They had fought the German Christians on the basis of the confession of faith, and now they had some hard theological work to do on writing a Confession. Bodelschwingh was asked to invite a small group of younger theologians to work on this. The assignment was to work out together, in the seclusion of Bodelschwingh's institute, a 'modern confession of faith'. Bonhoeffer and Sasse worked in this group during the second half of August 1933 and wrote a 'confession' which the others more or less approved. This was serious theological work, not interconfessional controversy. Inevitably, the result looked Lutheran! It was based upon six classical points of the Lutheran doctrine of the church, but it took up the points being made by the Reformed churches, particularly as outlined by Karl Barth.

A glance at the content of the Bethel Confession is enough to show that this was a serious attempt to keep the doctrines of the church from being misused. Chapter 1 dealt with the authority of the Bible and stressed its totality, including the Old Testament. It was a redefinition of the unique authority of Holy Scripture. Chapter 2 attacked the *völkisch*-nationalist misuse of Luther and the Reformation. Chapter 3 affirmed the doctrine of the Trinity, resisting any kind of independent doctrine of creation. Chapter 4, on 'Creation and Sin', took up this theme in more detail and developed the teaching of Karl Barth, making a significant theological statement:

> We recognize the Creator only through obedience to the Word of God from Scripture, not through any interpretation of events in the world . . . Therefore we reject the heresy that God speaks directly to us from a particular 'historical hour' . . . the heresy that the voice of the people is the voice of God. The voice of the people cries, 'Hosanna' and 'Crucify him'.[28]

Chapter 6 was on the 'Holy Spirit of the Church'. With this chapter, the confession ended its *implied* reference to the events of the day and came to *direct* reference in the last three sections, which were: 'Church and *Volk*', 'Church and State', and 'Church and the Jews'.

Much of the earlier chapters was written into the Barmen Declaration in 1934; but these last three sections were rejected. Years later, Barth confessed that they were wrong to be silent about the Jews, but added,

> But then, such a text would not have been acceptable to either the Reformed or the General Synod, given the spiritual predisposition of even the 'Confessing Church' in 1934 . . . But this does not excuse the fact that I . . . did not offer at least formal resistance in this matter at that time.[29]

With the rejection of his draft at Bethel, Bonhoeffer recognised far deeper divisions than the division between Lutheran and Reformed, and perhaps deeper than those which divided Catholic from Protestant. Later, in the church struggle, he could easily tolerate a Confessing Church which included Lutheran and Reformed, but not German Christians. The real division was not on theoretical doctrines, but on willingness to speak the truth in Nazi Germany. So sure was he of this that he tried to convince the ecumenical movement that only the Confessing Church should represent Germany, and he was prepared to say, 'Outside the Confessing Church, there is no salvation.'

THE ECUMENICAL MOVEMENT

Bonhoeffer was a critical supporter of the ecumenical movement. His main criticism was that it had not developed a theology. This was not a call for an excluding theological statement, but for a new birth of theological earnestness related to the issues of the day. He also criticised the ecumenical movement for not acting upon its strength in the matter of an international call for peace. But even as a youth secretary, he saw the falling away of denominational shibboleths. In prison he wrote of 'antiquated controversies'.

Bonhoeffer looked to a World Council of Churches and to an ecumenical council which could speak with authority to the nations of the world. In his appeal for a call of peace at Fanö in 1934, he said:

> Why do we fear the fury of the world powers? Why don't we take the power from them and give it back to Christ? We can still do it today. The Ecumenical Council is in session [a rhetorical exaggeration for so small and only partially representative a conference]; it can send out to all believers this radical call to peace. The nations are waiting for it in the East and in the West. Must we be put to shame by non-Christian people in the East? [He had Gandhi's India in mind.] Shall we desert the individuals who are risking their lives for this message? The hour is late. The world is choked with weapons, and dreadful is the distrust which looks out of all men's eyes. The trumpets of war may blow tomorrow. For what are we waiting? Do we want to become involved in this guilt as never before? . . . We want to give the world a whole word, not a half word – a courageous word, a Christian word. We want to pray that this word may be given us today. Who knows if we shall see each other again another year?[30]

That was in 1934. He had already abandoned the 'antiquated controversies' and turned as preacher and theologian to stirring up the courage of a universal church. It was three years after his death that the World Council of Churches was formed in Amsterdam, 1948. Its theme was 'God's Order and Man's Disorder'. Many of the antiquated controversies were still voiced there; but the slogan of this first assembly was, '*We intend to stay together.*'

This is no place to write the history of the ecumenical movement, but at certain points in the chequered story of the WCC, the plea of Bonhoeffer has been heard. In 1952, at the World Conference on Faith and Order at Lund in Sweden, the formula was propounded that the member-churches should do *together* everything that deep differences of conviction did not compel them to do *separately*. In 1966, the Church and Society Conference gave voice to the oppressed and led eventually to the setting up of a special fund to combat racism. Although this led to controversy, it also led to action. The South African Council of Churches has declared the need to draw up a Confession which would condemn racism as a heresy.

Bonhoeffer has found his followers in distant lands, including Japan, where a 'declaration of guilt' by the churches has been framed upon the German Stuttgart Statement of 1945. More recently, his call for peace at Fanö has been re-echoed at the Evangelischer Kirchentag and at a WCC Assembly in Vancouver. And all these things have channelled into the world concern for 'Justice, Peace and Integrity of Creation'. In all this, denominational differences have been slight. The demand for an Ecumenical Council has raised some differences about the word 'Council', but the need for the churches to get together on a theological study and a public utterance that the world can hear reminds us of Bonhoeffer's words, 'the day will come when men will once more be called so to utter the word of God that the world will be changed and renewed by it'.[31] But that is beginning to lead us into the third part of this book.

Part 3

Consequences for the Future of the Church

INTRODUCTION

Bonhoeffer's insights concerning the maturity of the person and the relevance of such historical development for the future of the church itself and in the relation to the world are of great significance. What has happened since shows that his insights were fundamentally right. This does not mean that he was right in every particular, and it is important that we should not regard him as an infallible authority.

Bonhoeffer was a Christian man of remarkable honesty, courage and integrity, in a time and under circumstances which brought the issues of world and church into bright focus. He was a theologian of some eminence, and he did not hesitate to pursue the path along which his experience and his thinking led him. He was also given time at the end of his short life to consider without day-to-day responsibilities the logic of his thought. He had the added advantage that he could write down his thoughts in terms of a conversation with a close friend, who was himself an eminent theologian. The circumstances of his life also illustrated a person who was prepared to accept the consequences of his beliefs. He would not have described his tragic death as a martyrdom, but with hindsight, we may call him a martyr.

Bonhoeffer was out of step with the accommodating theology of his day and ruthless in his criticism of any theology which was not authentic. This made him something of an exile. Therefore Eberhard Bethge, in a book from which we have already quoted, chose the title *Bonhoeffer: Exile and Martyr.*[1] An exile can often see his country more clearly than those who live through difficult times in it. Bonhoeffer refused the luxury of exile from Germany when he returned from America in 1939; but he remained an exile from contemporary German theology when he chose the path of life that led to his execution. He wanted to be in Germany when the time came to reconstruct. He prepared himself for this, but his martyrdom robbed him of this opportunity – and robbed Germany of one of its most powerful Christian leaders. That same martyrdom gave him the right to be heard. Gradually his thoughts have influenced post-war theology in Germany and throughout the world.

In the first two parts of this book we have traced the way in which many of Bonhoeffer's thoughts have been taken up along the lines he indicated in his 'Outline for a Book'.[2] Not all have been taken up, and not all have proved important, but it was right to take them all seriously. Now in this third part, by the nature of the material, the 'Outline' is less helpful.

Bonhoeffer was looking at the consequences for the immediate post-war world. It may be that if we had heeded him then, we might have had a more relevant church today. But in many important points we did not. This is most clearly brought out in a remarkable journal called *Kirchliche Zeitgeschichte* ('Contemporary Church History'), the third issue of which was devoted to the church in the years immediately following the Second World War (1945–1948).[3] The articles in it originated as papers given at a conference held in Potsdam in August 1988. They were from historians, sociologists, theologians, *etc.*, who had made a special study in their own countries of what had happened to the church in those three years after war had ended and occupying troops had withdrawn. The countries were almost all in a Europe which had been involved in war – Germany, Hungary, Czechoslovakia, France, Denmark and Germany itself, East and West as well as Austria. It soon became clear that the churches under communist control had heeded Bonhoeffer's 'consequences' far more than those in the West. The third part of his 'Outline' was relevant, whether heeded or not, in all the countries of Europe. But that was the period 1945–1948. Now, forty years after that, it is a different picture, and there are consequences that Bonhoeffer had not thought of, and some of his consequences are no longer valid.

9

CONSEQUENCES FOR THE FUTURE OF THE CHURCH

THE CHURCH IS THE CHURCH ONLY WHEN IT EXISTS FOR OTHERS

Our medieval heritage has left us with a remnant of division. The church is the church and the world is the world. The relationship between the two is paradoxical. It is often summed up in a garbled account of Jesus' prayer for his disciples in John 17. The disciples, and therefore the church, are '*in* the world, and yet not *of* the world'. Thus, the world is alien: 'Here we have no abiding city.' And the church's attitude to the world is to correct it, rescue people from its evil influence, watch it lest it should creep into the church like a camel coming into the tent, defend the church from it, and many other such strategies that imply a certain hostility. Thus, for example, evangelism on this model consists of offering to the world something which it does not have, but which the church does possess.

If Bonhoeffer is to be listened to, evangelism is not such a one-way affair, nor is it the conquest of the world by the church. It is participation with others. It means allowing God to develop a relationship between the church and world. This allows for what Ronald Gregor Smith refers to as the new creation of a new form of human community,[1] so that evangelism renews the church as well as the world. The church is 'community' both in its purpose and in the means it uses to achieve that purpose. Ronald Gregor Smith developed this by linking Martin Buber's understanding of human life as 'encounter' with Paul Tillich's insistence that God is 'the ground of our being'. God is the ground of all participation, whether it be Gorbachev and the West or an ecumenical conference. The two are not all that different, as the Fourth Assembly of the World Council of Churches at Uppsala showed. The very simple conclusion from these thoughts is that the world is as much the sphere of the Holy Spirit as the church is.

If this were taken seriously, the church would have no frontiers with the world. Privileges, power, wealth, influence are not attributes of the church at all. In very simple form, it is put in a joke about a pope who watches the riches of the Vatican being moved to a new palace. He comments, 'Unlike my predecessor, I cannot say, "Silver and gold, have I none."' To which his chaplain replies, 'No, neither can you say, "rise up and walk"'! There was a lowering of the frontiers of the church to let wealth in. And this is not confined to the Roman Catholic Church. The church resists worldly habits such as trading on Sundays, but accumulates wealth and influence.

Bonhoeffer said to his own church that the first step towards being the church for the world was to sell its possessions and give to the poor. He also advocated that the clergy should be supported by the free-will offerings of the worshippers. In Bonhoeffer's Germany that meant saying that the 'church tax' should be abolished; in the contemporary Church of England, it would mean giving away its medieval endowments and accumulated wealth and letting the congregations pay for their clergy if they want them! The German churches in the Federal Republic (West Germany) restored the church tax as soon as they could. In the German Democratic Republic (East Germany) the tax was phased out and the churches were paid only for the social work they were doing for the state. This is still true. The effect is noticeable in the relative opulence of the churches in the West – including Switzerland and Scandinavia. The American churches, separating church and state, have learnt how to support their churches by tithing. They too are opulent. Even in Britain, where this opulence is not so evident, the churches show signs of being the preserve of a 'comfortable' class.

In recent years this latter point has become sufficient of a scandal to bring the Church of England into something like class warfare! *Faith in the City*,[2] the report of the Archbishop's Commission on Urban Priority Areas, revealed the extent of poverty in Britain and the lack of resources in urban areas. The government was quick to point out that the church was meddling in affairs which did not concern it. Those who spoke in this way had often read only those parts of the report that criticised the government for not supplying adequate resources, if they read it at all. Most of the report was a criticism of the church. It has led not to selling all and giving to the poor, but to a nationwide audit of the resources of the churches and the setting up of an urban fund to 'give to the poor', or enable the church to be more effective in relieving the misery of so many people's lives.

This marks the beginning of an acceptance of the fact that the resources of the church do not belong to the church, but are for the world. This has to be worked out with more than money or property. The spiritual gifts are also for the world. The person who speaks in tongues on Sunday and curses his neighbour on Monday has forgotten this. A healing service which brings glory to the church must be followed up by caring for the social conditions in which the healed person has to continue to live. These are but minor examples of abuses, where the church is tempted to act as though the Spirit of God poured out his riches upon the church and then the church out of its abundance contributed something to those outside. The basic consequence of regarding the church as 'for the world' is that, like the God whom it worships, the church loves the world and gives itself for it. Such a church could not judge the world, nor should it desire to, but would seek to renew it. In the midst of injustice and war, exploitation and cruelty, where humanity has lost its way and is destroying itself, the church shares the suffering and the ignominy and points to Christ suffering too. The purpose of the church is to be in the world like leaven in dough, not like the cook shaping cakes! The church 'stands by God in his hour of grieving'.[3]

The liberation theologians have done this. Antonio Pérez-Esclarín, a Jesuit from Venezuela, was an intellectual. His last book, *Atheism and Liberation*,[4] showed the intellectual resources of the church used in the service of artists, writers, philosophers and theologians. It was also a hard-hitting book:

> Neither atheism nor faith is worth anything if it remains mere ideology. Each must be something more than sterile talk and an intellectual exercise. God is with those committed to the cause of justice, not with those who merely sing or talk about it. Atheists and Christians are on the side of authentic religion and God if they are committed to the cause of justice and love in the world. They are against religion and God if they help to maintain injustice and lack of love.[5]

Many Jesuits in Latin America would agree with him. And for one glorious moment in 1968, at Medellín in Colombia, the South American bishops accepted this kind of talk and action. Archbishop Romero was gunned down at the altar for it. There may be many ways of being committed to the cause of justice, and the Jesuit movement is one easily recognised as the church existing for the world. This is not just Christian priests becoming Marxists and encouraging revolution. This is committed Christians feeling the pain of Christ in the world, seeing his face in the face of the starving and oppressed. They have acted, gone among the people and suffered with them, felt their anger and made it their own. Antonio Pérez-Esclarín has a postscript to his book which is a good parable for the church, abandoning its self-preservation and the idols of 'church growth' in order to be the church existing for the world:

> My readers, if there are any readers, will probably find this book hasty, unequal and poorly worked out. I must confess that while I was writing it, I felt an enormous desire to leave it in mid-course. I felt that these were just words, when the only worthwhile thing is committed personal action with the people. I finished the book hurriedly, overcoming myself continually, thinking that perhaps it might help someone after all. I feel no desire at all to go back over it and touch it up. Furthermore, I want these lines to be my final goodbye to the intellectual world. I have felt its attractions, but I think I have discovered its phoniness. Every idea is hollow if

it is not fleshed out in real life. I don't know whether the book I have written is of any value. But as for myself, I am going to try to live out its contents with the oppressed.[6]

In the situation of Latin America, the consequences of what Bonhoeffer says are liberation theology and the kind of action with the people that many Jesuits and others have been compelled to take. In the situation of an archbishop in England, who has to preach after a victory such as we had in the Falklands, it is to say what he is constrained by the gospel to say, regardless of government disapproval. Any bishop of Durham would have had to speak out about the plight of miners during a cruel strike. Desmond Tutu has to be a voice for those who will not be heard in South Africa. And the churches in Germany who in a previous generation aided the glorification of war and now see the awful escalation of nuclear weapons are right to stand with the young people of the peace movement. As they watch the treatment of 'guest-workers' from Turkey and Iran, they are right to identify with them in their distress. When they see the pollution of the Rhine, the destruction of the forests and the dangers in the atmosphere, they are in sympathy with a suffering creation. It is very much a consequence of Bonhoeffer's thought about the church that its deepest concern should be with justice, peace and the integrity of creation. In this the church is for the world. The church is more truly the church at the Council of Basel (1989), demanding with the people a better world, than when it is defending the doctrine of the Trinity or the virgin birth. 'The church must share in the secular problems of ordinary human life.'[7]

THE MAN FOR OTHERS

The church is all-embracing, excluding none. The word is preached, the sacraments are offered, and around these mysteries a community is gathered which the Holy Spirit forms into a *koinonia*, or fellowship. But only those who walk away are excluded. This is no close fellowship of the elite. It is a part of the world. And in that world Christ suffers.

After all these centuries, I wonder if a familiar story from the gospels would be written differently. When Christ asked the disciples, 'Who do men say that I am?', how would they answer today? Perhaps, 'Some say you are the second person of the Trinity, of one substance with the Father; others say that they can't understand what that means, but think you far above their heads and out of their experience; others say that you never existed.' And then the decisive question to the church: 'But who do you say that I am?' And our answer has to be carefully considered.

This was Bonhoeffer's continuing question. Jesus had posed the question in two stages: 'What is the popular opinion?' and 'What is your conviction?' Consciously or not, Bonhoeffer followed this posing of the question in stages. Because he could not regard the question as academic, but only in an existential form – *i.e.*, not 'What *should* I believe?' but 'What *do I* believe?' – Bonhoeffer began with 'Who am I?' An authentic faith is based upon a person who believes, not a historic creed.

In prison, Bonhoeffer was aware that he had built a reputation for coolness in the face of danger, and for haughtiness in dealing with his jailers. He brought this out most clearly in his poem 'Who am I?'[8]

> Who am I? They often tell me
> I would step from my cell's confinement
> calmly, cheerfully, firmly,
> like a squire from his country-house.

There is much else 'which other men tell of', but it does not correspond with his own feelings:

Am I then really all that which other men tell of?
Or am I only what I know of myself,
restless and longing and sick, like a bird in a cage,
struggling for breath, as though hands were compressing
   my throat,
yearning for colours, for flowers, for the voices of birds,
thirsting for words of kindness, for neighbourliness,
trembling with anger at despotisms and petty humiliation,
tossing in expectation of great events,

powerlessly trembling for friends at an infinite distance,
weary and empty at praying, at thinking, at making,
faint, and ready to say farewell to it all?

The contrast has to be resolved. Is it due to hypocrisy or
vacillation, or is there a contradiction in himself –

> . . . like a beaten army,
> fleeing in disorder from victory already achieved?

The ambiguities and the questions trouble him:

Who am I? They mock me, these lonely questions of mine.

He can only reconcile the contradictions in a kind of agnos-
ticism followed by confidence:

> Whoever I am, thou knowest, O God, I am thine.

And part of this statement includes the fact that we cannot
understand ourselves or our relation to God without taking
into account our solidarity with others.

That means also our solidarity of guilt, and this is most
clearly worked out in his long poem 'Night Voices in Tegel'.[9]
The poem begins with the sentiment of 'Who am I?':

> Outside, a summer evening
> That does not know me
> Goes singing into the countryside.[10]

Soon, the sounds of prison guards, the hidden laughter of two
lovers, the silent night thoughts of fellow prisoners and
various sounds from within the prison draw him into a solidarity with humanity. He feels the darkness of the night and
hears its voice:

> 'I am not dark; only guilt is dark!'[11]

What follows is the acceptance of guilt. The poem leads
directly to the Stuttgart Declaration in 1945 of the Evangelical
Churches of Germany, a statement signed by the heroes of
the Resistance. The consequences historically were slight,
but twenty years later led to the Japanese Declaration, by
churches who recognised that they had not identified them-

selves enough with the sufferings of the world and thus shared in the guilt which caused that suffering. It would have been good if the churches of the victorious allies had more clearly acknowledged their shared guilt. While at Nuremberg, no one from the victorious side was convicted or even tried as a war criminal. Despite Hiroshima and Nagasaki, there was no equivalent to the Stuttgart Declaration of Guilt by the churches. This moral defect has had its consequences in the collapse of moral values in post-war years and perhaps also in the decline of the churches in the West. Individuals, of course, felt and expressed this sense of shared guilt.

More immediately, Bonhoeffer showed that he could not understand himself unless he recognised his solidarity of guilt:

> 'We sons of pious races,
> One-time defenders of right and truth,
> Became despisers of God and man,
> Amid hellish laughter.'[12]

The events of 1933–1945 have left us all aware of the relevance of such lines, and we respond to the later words of the poem:

> 'Brother, till the night be past,
> Pray for [us]!'[13]

The poem does not end in gloom, however:

> Outside a summer morning
> Which is not yet mine
> Goes brightly into the countryside.[14]

The consequence of a solidarity of guilt is not despair, but hope.

Jürgen Moltmann has shown the truth of this last point in many of his writings.[15] Dorothee Sölle, in her book, *Choosing Life*,[16] ends her key chapter on 'Christ – The Dignity of Men and Women' with her own confession of this:

I am a Christian if I believe that everything is possible. The blind learn how to see, old Nazis stop suppressing their past, technocrats listen to the powerless. The lame walk, the deaf hear, the poor hear the news of liberation . . . I am a Christian because I believe that what was promised to everyone is possible.

Jesus of Nazareth tried to do with his life something that I want to do too, something which is for me really all important . . .

He is my brother who, since he is a little older than me, is always a death ahead of me; who, since he is a little younger than me, and madder than me, is always a miracle ahead of me.

What does he do for me? I learn from him . . . He talks about my life in the way I want him to talk, without any contempt. He doesn't allow a single day of my life to be held cheap, doesn't allow it to be meaningless or without the great experiment. I learn from him to overcome all cynicism. I find this the most difficult lesson today. For there are convincing reasons for despising people. There are excellent reasons for despising myself. There is a temptation to affirm life only partially, for only a little way, only under certain circumstances. He puts me to shame – my limited, impatient, partly superficial affirmation. He teaches me an infinite, a revolutionary 'yes' which doesn't leave out anything or anybody at all.[17]

The importance of Dorothee Sölle's book lies in her attitude to our world, which she can compare with the world in which her parents grew up in Nazi Germany – Bonhoeffer's world. She sees the need for the church to recognise its guilt of involvement in class war, materialism, racism, sexism and all the other blindnesses and violences we are prone to in our day. Speaking at the Goethe Institute in London, at about the time when her book appeared, she summed up the disease of our day as 'consumer fascism'. She called upon all Christians to recognise their responsibility for it and do something. She told of how as a girl, when she first heard of the terrible events of Nazi Germany, she asked her parents, 'What did you do?' and they turned away without answering. 'I do not want my children to say to me in years to come, "What did you do?" in relation to the consumer fascism of our day, and I can only turn away without an answer.'

That diversion into Dorothee Sölle is not irrelevant to Bonhoeffer's question 'Who is Jesus Christ for us today?' Like Bonhoeffer, we can answer it only in relation to an understanding of ourselves and our solidarity of guilt with our generation. We are not innocent, standing in a guilty world. The church does not protect us from guilt. Church and world are together in their guilt, and together they must be reconciled to God.

The classic statement that in Christ 'God was reconciling the world to himself' (2 Corinthians 5:19) is the key to our understanding of Jesus Christ. This he is still for us today. As part of the world, but a special part of the world, we are reconciled. In choosing his disciples Jesus did not look for innocent followers. He chose sinners, and their reconciliation was a slow and incomplete process. Paul saw the process as going on until the very end of time, when God would reconcile all frustrated nature to his purpose. But just as Paul saw humanity redeemed in order that the creation may attain its purpose, so we may see the church used as a pioneer of redemption for the world. This is not to say that the church has already achieved, but that it is witnessing to the process.

That passage in Romans 8 confirms Bonhoeffer's view that the Bible talks not of individual salvation, but of communities being redeemed. Salvation has become less important as a personal experience determining our condition in the after-life than as a process by which this world is changed. In his letter of 5 May 1944,[18] Bonhoeffer begins to look at this:

> What does it mean to 'interpret in a religious sense'? I think it means to speak on the one hand metaphysically, and on the other hand individualistically. Neither of these is relevant to the biblical message or to the man of today. Hasn't the individualistic question about personal salvation almost completely left us all? Aren't we really under the impression that there are more important things than that question (perhaps not more important than the *matter* itself, but more important than the *question*!)? I know it sounds pretty monstrous to say that. But, fundamentally, isn't this in fact biblical? Does the question about saving one's soul appear in the Old Testament at all? Aren't righteousness and the Kingdom of God on earth the focus of everything? And isn't it true that Rom. 3.24ff. is not an individualistic doctrine of salvation, but the culmination of the view that God alone is righteous?[19]

That last point is important enough to make us pause. The passage in Romans is closely argued. Beginning at Romans

3:21, the statement which controls the argument is that 'the righteousness of God has been manifested apart from law'. Of course, 'the law and the prophets bear witness to it', but 'the righteousness of God through faith in Jesus Christ' is available to 'all who believe', not just those who have lived correctly under the law. This is because 'all have sinned' – those who have tried to live by the law and those who are without the law. All 'are justified by [God's] grace' – as a gift, 'through the redemption which is in Christ Jesus'. This is the process, proving that God alone is righteous and justifies all who have faith in Jesus (Romans 3:21–26). On that basis, Bonhoeffer continues: 'It is not with the beyond that we are concerned, but with this world as created and preserved, subjected to laws, reconciled, and restored. What is above this world is, in the gospel, intended to exist *for* this world.'[20] Bonhoeffer does not mean this in a liberal or mystical sense, but in a truly biblical one. It is in this sense that he bids us understand the creation, and the incarnation, crucifixion and resurrection of Jesus Christ as *for* this world.

It is on this basis that Bonhoeffer would have us examine the necessity of the church sharing in the secular problems of ordinary human life. In this, the church does not dominate, but helps and serves. The government has no right to tell the church not to meddle in politics, but it can tell the church that it is wrong or incompetent. Traditionally, but not always consistently, the church has warned governments of the consequences of their wrongdoing. But it has often done this from a superior moral position. It has not always remembered that 'judgement begins at the house of God'.

A neglect of the Old Testament has often meant forgetting the example of God's ancient people the Jews, who were more severely judged because they were God's people. Amos, for example, judged the nations for their crimes against humanity, but God's people for their silence and lack of faith. A good example of the chastened church making known God's condemnation of crimes against humanity was found in 1989, when the Anglican Church of Japan called upon its members to refrain from ceremonies at the funeral of the Emperor, not only because of the evil he had led in the war and the massacre of prisoners in his name, but because they themselves had been silent and even been used to glorify an evil regime.

It is the chastened church which appreciates a government and calls upon it to do right. The cry is not '*You* have sinned!', but '*We* have sinned.' This acceptance of a solidarity of guilt underlines the importance of example. Human example has its origin in the humanity of Jesus. The power of the church and the effectiveness of the word of the church lies not in abstract arguments, but in its example.

Stephen Neill, towards the end of his book *Crises of Belief*[21], has highlighted this in terms of relations with other faiths. He has described the activities of many churches, 'doing a great deal of house-cleaning, and preparing themselves, though still very inadequately, for their tasks in the modern world'.[22] He then asks how Christians can enter into dialogue with those of other faiths. And throughout Europe this is a live question. Hendrik Kraemer, whom he reports, had said that the first requisite of a Christian ambassador must be an 'open congenial understanding' of the other faiths.[23] But 'the message of Jesus Christ is proclamation, challenge, and judgment'. We cannot come to other faiths today as dogmatists or critics, but in a spirit of humble questioning, 'entitled to ask our questions, because we have first submitted ourselves to theirs'.[24]

An excellent example of this was given in 1988, when Christians were offended by the showing of the film *The Last Temptation of Christ*[25] and Muslims were deeply offended by the prominence given to a novel submitted for the Booker Prize, Salman Rushdie's *The Satanic Verses*.[26] The Muslim scholars in the Regent's Park Mosque invited Christian leaders to a day of hospitality and discussion. Each tried to understand the offence, and in that atmosphere of mutual concern talked of one another's faith. One was reminded of Kenneth Cragg's words, 'Only a person of faith can understand the faith of another.'

Stephen Neill maintains that there are two questions that Christians are compelled to ask in their dialogue with other faiths: 'Have those of other faiths "ever really heard of a God who acts"?', and 'Have they "ever really looked at Jesus Christ and tried to see him as he is?" '[27] In the atmosphere of that mosque, it can be said that those of Islam who felt the hurt of their friends and compared it with their own really looked at Jesus as he is. It may not change their lives. The good work done was shattered by the call of the Ayatollah Khomeini to kill Salman Rushdie by whatever means and the offer of a reward to whoever accomplished it, Muslim or not. The persistent attempts of Christian leaders in London, Manchester, Bradford and wherever there were large population of Muslims, to express sympathy with the hurt, prevented any large scale acceptance of the Ayatollah's horrendous decree. Muslim/Christian relations are slowly being repaired despite, and perhaps because of, the inhuman decree of Khomeini. But we who are believers and ask one of another faith or of no faith at all to look at Jesus, cannot say, 'Look at him, but do not look at us.' The messenger of the gospel is identified by his hearers, not only with his message, but with his God: Dr Vicedom, who writes from experience as a missionary in New Guinea, says powerfully:

> God comes to the people through His messengers. It is by their behaviour that God is judged. If the missionaries succeed in entering into the life of the people, in adapting themselves to their way of living, if they learn the language and become in many ways the advisers, friends and helpers of the Papuans, gradually confidence in the missionaries is established. This confidence is at once transferred to God. God is always judged in the light of what the missionaries are. Unless this comes to pass, even in New Guinea we shall hear people say, 'Your God is a foreign God. He demands new ways of doing things. He speaks our language so badly that it makes us sick even to listen to you.'[28]

And that is not only true in New Guinea. The great words of our faith, however interpreted, will not renew the world if they are too closely associated with inauthentic human examples.

John Bowden in his book *Jesus: The Unanswered Questions*[29] set out on a perilous journey with a passionate faith, facing the unanswered questions about Jesus. He did not get all the answers, but he had to ask the questions, and he had to match his partial and provisional answers with authentic action. Then in the last pages – difficult, because they can never be the last – he saw that there was more than questions and action:

> Those who identify themselves with the movement that began with Jesus, and indeed those of other faiths would also want to say, as I do, that what we do, our questions and our actions, are sometimes met with that which, the One who, comes to us from beyond ourselves, that to which, or the One to whom, traditional talk of the grace and love of God refers. That it is difficult to talk about this in our language, in our world, does not mean that it does not happen. We can experience it, and hear accounts of experience of it from those who are not confessedly Christians as well as those who are. That is something which changes the whole picture for those who are unaware of this dimension.[30]

Then Bowden raises a question which Bonhoeffer also raises at the very end of his 'Outline for a Book'. Bowden suggests that we may have to look beyond 'the Christian liturgy with all the current malaise surrounding liturgical worship'.[31] He himself found such help in his compilation of the riches of Jewish and Christian liturgical traditions in his book *By Heart*,[32] which he claims is a companion volume to his *Jesus: The Unanswered Questions*. And he ends the latter with a Collect from the Book of Common Prayer.

Bonhoeffer ends his 'Outline' with a short list of reforms needed in the liturgical practices of the church and its preparation for serving the world. He talks of revising the creeds (the Apostles' Creed), of the need for a new kind of apologetics, the need for reform in the training of ministers and for a new pattern of life for the clergy. He recognises that all this is too condensed and perhaps a little crude, but here are certain things he wants to say *simply* and *clearly*.[33]

Although Bethge recognises that these remarks are provisional and says that Bonhoeffer knew this, he asks whether there was a reason why he should mention these three things especially as in need of revision – creed, apologetics and ministry. Perhaps he thought they acted as barriers and roadblocks in their present form. Bethge continues, 'They are ancient dogmatic fixations of the church acting as religion; the church keeps and protects them and thus allows the preaching of the Gospel to be obscured. Thus, the discovery of the "church for others" and "Jesus for others" is also thwarted.'[34]

THE CREEDS

The history of the use and misuse of creeds throughout the centuries is enough to justify Bonhoeffer's concern. Clearly, he was not suggesting a rewriting of the creeds, or the finding of additional creeds to add to the burden of the earlier ones. He was questioning the creeds as such.

The value of creeds was early recognised as a memorable summary of the main points of the gospel or *Kerygma*. The association with baptism was obvious. A young person coming out of paganism or from a Jewish background needed to know what the gospel was all about. They were baptised because they acknowledged Jesus as Lord. It was the way the Master went and commanded. The disciple followed him through the waters of baptism. But there was much to learn, and before the gospels were written down the creeds served as convenient summaries. There were no doubt other things to learn – for example, the procedure at the Lord's Supper, as quoted by Paul in 1 Corinthians 11, and the evidence for the resurrection from the appearances to witnesses of the Lord after his death, quoted by Paul in 1 Corinthians 15.

Letters, creeds and statements of faith became the subject of controversy at ecumenical councils. They were used to define orthodoxy and refute heresy. They became polemical statements for which men would die and kill. Their peaceful use in modern liturgical practice disguises their bitter history. But even in the liturgy they are often substitutes for faith or protections against doubt. The creeds of the church can be accepted, repeated and venerated without necessarily being believed. Behind their ancient sacredness we hide the question of what we really believe. The doubts are repressed and worship proceeds wrapped in the clothes of old controversies, which do not fit our way of thinking.

Whatever we do with our worship in the new age, it is unlikely to need the historic creeds. And before we ask how they can be replaced, we must ask what a creed is for. The first Christians came declaring in triumph that Jesus was Lord. That was all their creed. It was a shout of triumph, not a doctrinal statement. They read the 'memoirs' of the apostles because they thirsted to know of the earthly life of him who revealed God to them. Theological arguments belonged in debate or controversy, while the creeds that emerged were statements to be defended.

Should our creeds not express our knowledge of God and our experience of his working in our lives? In those creeds we should discover who Jesus Christ is for us today, we should learn how we stand by God in his grieving, how we identify with Christ in the world as the church for others. We are not ready to write these words yet, but the ancient creeds will not do, because we have misused them to separate ourselves from our brethren and sisters in the world. They have silenced questioning too long, and strangled honest doubt. Bonhoeffer was right to call for a revision of the creeds – and yet I can see no way in which they can be rewritten. Perhaps they have to be, 'Drawn out in living characters'.[35]

CHRISTIAN APOLOGETICS

The confident apologetics of the nineteenth century missionaries have gone. The Christian can no longer face the person of another faith, or no faith at all, with such confidence as to believe that all he has to do is point out the errors and correct them from a position of certainty. The Christian today seeks with the seeker. There is, of course, a confidence. The person who has seen the truth of God in Jesus is pledged to do the truth. Such a person will grow in understanding and will find points where he or she can stand without compromise, 'not tossed about by every wind of doctrine'. Yet the approach to other forms of human faith must be marked by the deepest humility. Stephen Neill, in his *Crises of Belief*, spells this out:

[The Christian] must endeavour to meet [the other forms of human faith] at their highest, and not cheaply to score points off them by comparing the best he knows in his own faith with their weaknesses, weaknesses such as are present also in the Christian scheme as it is lived out by very imperfect Christians. He must, as far as imagination will permit, expose himself to the full force of these other faiths in all that they have that is most convincing and most alluring. He must rejoice in everything that they possess of beauty and high aspiration. He must put himself to school with them, in readiness to believe that they may have something to teach him that he has not yet learned. He must sympathise with their earnest efforts to relate themselves to the needs of men in the modern world. He must listen with respectful patience to every criticism that they have to make both of Christian thought and Christian practice.[36]

Stephen Neill has there given the atmosphere and attitude of modern Christian apologetics. It means the end of triumphalism, and it requires a willingness to receive the treasures of other faiths. And other cultures and ideologies must be included. Of course, this does not mean a total relativism or that all religions are equally good. Christianity by its very nature has total claims, but they are the claims of Christ, not of the church.

In that same book, Stephen Neill has tried to provide the confident setting for Christian apologetics. He lays down three categories.[37]

1. While human thought sways between *realism* (the view that all is explained in terms of this visible world) and *idealism* (that this visible world only exists in the mind of the observer), the Christian must think in terms of a real world which is so dependent upon the beyond that it is never completely explained in terms of this world. Bonhoeffer repeatedly insists that we must live in the real world and may not opt out to explain. But that there is more than this real world must also be accepted. God is not contained within the world, although he suffers within it.

2. The Christian can think only in terms of purpose. Many of his most poignant problems would be solved if he could give meaninglessness to the universe. Jacques Monod[38] has opted for this: a Christian thinker cannot. Man is able to form

a purpose and to maintain his effort towards it despite frustration and failure.

'The purpose of God is one of the postulates of Christian thinking.'[39] Christian apologetics must take this into account. This postulate does not always help us in answering awkward questions about God's activity or lack of it in the world, as C. S. Lewis discovered in the introductory chapter to his *The Problem of Pain*:

> [Christianity] is not a system into which we have to fit the awkward fact of pain: it is itself one of the awkward facts which have to be fitted into any system we make. In a sense, it creates, rather than solves, the problem of pain, for pain would be no problem unless, side by side with our daily experience of this painful world, we had received what we think a good assurance that ultimate reality is righteous and loving.[40]

This attitude influenced the nature of Lewis's Christian apologetics. Since his time, the sense of purpose in our understanding of the world has been greatly strengthened by the writings of Teilhard de Chardin.[41] Even a scientist like Paul Davies can conclude without necessarily accepting Christian doctrine that there appears to be something going on behind the universe.[42]

3. History is the sphere in which God chooses to operate. Events happen, and once they have happened no power can unmake them. There is thus a reliability about history that we cannot gainsay. The effect of this upon Christian apologetics is that faith is rooted in the historical. Theology cannot have a special logic. If we are to attempt to show the reality of the resurrection, it has to be done in historical terms. Of course we cannot prove the resurrection historically, any more than we can prove the existence of God, but we have no escape clause in a historical argument with those of other faiths or none.

Within these three categories the problem of communicating the gospel is set. So far Stephen Neill has been helpful, but on Bonhoeffer's terms he fails at the jump when it comes to dealing with the 'secularist'. There, Neill is convinced that the secularist has to learn to ask the religious question, while

Bonhoeffer requires the Christian to follow the secularist argument and not opt out at the critical point. Christian apologetics cannot be conducted on the basis of moving the goal posts! The secularist asks his or her question legitimately when it is posed in secular terms, because they are the terms of the world in which we live. This does not mean that we have to prove the existence of God in secular terms. Long ago Pascal showed how foolish that was. But we have to talk about a God who is in the world. We have to discover him there, not bring him in. He does not fashion our world from outside. He comes into it, if the incarnation means anything, and there he remains with the power of love alone. His miracles are not the miracles of supernatural power, but the miracles of love. He suffers within our world, and we are called upon to stand by God in his hour of grieving. There are immense possibilities for Christian apologetics in these terms.

MINISTRY

All that has been attempted in this book leads us to a more than theological training for the ministry, to more than the training of priests to handle the holy mysteries. They will be called upon to do that, because the mysteries must be protected from profanation. The word must be preached, the sacraments celebrated and the *koinonia* which the Holy Spirit forms around word and sacrament made possible. But the minister must not be trained to a specialised and separate profession. He or she must be able to earn support by some other means, not only for economic reasons, but to bring the minister nearer to the people – within and without the church.

Such training is not for industrial chaplains, but for worker priests. The training to be a priest in the world is essential, rather than the training to be a priest separated from the world. Although the worker priests of France had a limited history and were 'recalled to their altars' by the authority of their church, we have much to learn from them. They arose out of the deep concern of the Roman Catholic Church in France and Belgium in particular, but they stimulated the church in many other countries and in many different confessions.

The limited history of the worker priests was precisely eleven years, from March 1943 to March 1954.[43] It began when, on 5 March 1943, the Abbés Godin and Daniel submitted to Cardinal Suhard, who was Archbishop of Paris, 'a memorandum on the conquest of the proletariat for Christianity'. These two Abbés had worked among young Christian workers and experienced the alienation of the 'working class' from the church. On the basis of ten years' experience, they gave an account of the almost complete dechristianisation of the working masses. The traditional methods of the church, they pointed out, were designed for a middle class – preaching, services, good works, *etc*. These 'do not catch hold of the masses', but 'turn those whom they do influence into bourgeoisie'. Thus implemented, the church's evangelism simply comprises a series of skirmishes to rescue people out of the industrial world. We make them like ourselves and have no real influence upon the industrial workers whom they have left behind. We are all aware of this danger: conversion so often pulls a person out of his or her world. Jesus had prayed that his disciples might not be taken out of this world. Yet we have persistently done so.

The Abbés Godin and Daniel proposed the formation of small Christian communities, independent of the parish churches, set down in the midst of the proletariat. Cardinal Suhard was sympathetic, and at first gave Abbé Godin a working-class parish for this experiment. But this did not work, and he finally commissioned him to train a team of priests. A few days later, the Assembly of Cardinals and Archbishops of France, faced with the refusal of the German Occupying Forces to permit chaplains to serve industrial workers in the armament factories, authorised twenty-five of the Abbé Godin's priests to join the industrial force as workers. They were mostly arrested and several died in concentration camps. In July, Cardinal Suhard founded the 'Mission de Paris', which relieved a team of priests from their regular duties to evangelise 'the common people of Paris and manual workers'. The priests worked in close liaison with

Christian laymen. This soon became a kind of liberation theology, when priests shared the conditions of the slave labourers of France and fought their battles. It was a revolution, and the church could not sustain it. Priests had given up their separation from the people. Their training then had to be quite different from the usual seminary training.

Bonhoeffer probably knew nothing of this movement, but it was some such identification with the world that led him to call for a new method of training ministers. His own experience in training ministers in Finkenwalde contributed to his desire for change.

In France the war ended and liberation brought new opportunities and the demands for a different kind of world. The worker priests were ready to take their place among the people of France as they sought to build a more just world. But the nearness to the people had meant a certain moving away from the hierarchy, particularly in Rome. The extent of Rome's concern can be seen in the nine questions put to Cardinal Suhard by the Congregation of the Holy Office in 1947:

> What is the rule of life, and what are the religious exercises, of the priests specially devoted to the service of the workers?
>
> Why is permission asked for evening celebration of the mass, even on weekdays?
>
> What advantages are expected from this form of apostolate, and what reasons are decisively in its favour?
>
> Are there not physical, moral and religious dangers to be apprehended?
>
> What precautions have you in mind?
>
> Could not the desired end be attained by means more in conformity with the priestly life?
>
> Are there not grounds for fearing that this method of apostolate may do harm by splitting the clergy into two parties in the eyes of the public, and by stressing the differences, too often cited, between the higher and inferior clergy?
>
> Certain regimes have brought in labour service, even for those in orders. Should a like claim be renewed, what ground would there be for protest if the same kind of work had already been undertaken voluntarily by men in orders?
>
> Will not this new form of apostolate damage the accustomed,

and necessary, ministry, as well as existing good works which have already given proof of their benevolence?[44]

That was an ecclesiastical bureaucracy getting worried. But soon there were more tangible reasons for concern. The worker priests had become so involved with the workers that they took part with them in a nationwide strike movement. The employers were becoming stronger: the resistance to German Occupation which had fashioned some kind of unity ended, and the anti-communist campaign was gathering strength. As later in Latin America, the priests were accused of being Marxists and teaching the same. The employers had at first looked upon the worker priests as their allies, who could be trusted to 'exercise a good influence' on the workers. But with their personal sharing of the living conditions of the workers, the worker priests took part in their battles!

Cardinal Suhard summed up his reasons for supporting the worker priests in a statement made in Notre Dame on the fiftieth anniversary of his ordination.

> To save the souls of Paris, that is the primary task. It is this multitude I will have to answer for on the Judgement Day. Now do you understand the anguish I suffer? It haunts me: it is an obsession that will not leave me. When I go through the suburbs with their gloomy factories, or the brightly lit streets of central Paris, I find the sight of the crowds, now elegant and now wretched, so heart-rending that it hurts me. I do not have to look far for a theme for my meditations. It is always the same – the wall dividing the Church from the masses. A wall that must at any cost be battered down in order to bring back Christ to the multitudes who have lost him. That is why we were glad to entrust·our *Mission de Paris* to certain of our priests, pioneers of the *avant garde*.[45]

In a total misunderstanding of that, the *Osservatore Romano* (the official newspaper of the Vatican) responded: 'A good Catholic does not go over to the enemy camp, deluded by the notion that he will be more effective there. On the contrary, he fulfils his duty among his own kind, without deserting.' There were other comments like that. The Roman Catholic Church took fright, and eventually the worker priests were recalled to their altars. Not all were obedient, but March 1954 saw the end of a hope.

I have discussed the worker priests at length because their case illustrates something of what might happen if we take Bonhoeffer seriously and train our priests and ministers for a different lifestyle.

The relative failure of the worker priests is a confirmation of Bonhoeffer's warning that a quick and ill-considered reform of the church would do no good. In fact the training for the ministry in all confessions has changed considerably since 1945, and the lifestyle of ministers has also changed along the lines of bringing them away from isolation and nearer to their flock. A recent report in America, outlining the success of evangelical churches with young people in comparison with Roman Catholic churches, sufficiently disturbed the Catholic bishops for them to ask if this success was due to the nearness of evangelical pastors to – and the remoteness of Catholic priests from – the everyday life of the young people.

Things have changed and are changing. But the resistance is still there. The privileged positions of the clergy are not easily given up – even if they are only assumed spiritual privileges.

EPILOGUE

The survival of the church has often been put in question by the shame and compromise of its leaders: a pope leading his troops into battle, bishops blessing guns, church resources enriched by the oppression of the poor, Lutheran pastors singing praises to Hitler as Saviour – and the sorry tale will go on. But always the church has survived in its shame.

Even more dramatically, it has survived the most bitter persecution. The epic period of the persecutions in the early church has become part of our church folklore and inspired many in times of trial. The Roman Catholic Church has derived succour from its saints and martyrs, the Protestants too have their *Book of Martyrs*.[1] In fact, the church handles persecution more effectively than it handles prosperity or popularity. Even in recent years, we have seen the church emerge strengthened from the years of persecution and near destruction in China. It is too early to say what the effect of anti-religious propaganda has been in the Soviet Union, but *glasnost* and *perestroika* have been like a spring to many minorities, and the Russian Orthodox Church has survived with all the splendour of her liturgy.

SURVIVAL IN THE WEST

Boredom and indifference have been greater dangers to the church in the West. The main effect has been the sense of irrelevance. Only occasionally is the church regarded with hostility, but the more familiar attitude has been that it is harmless and perhaps useful in the education of children and in support of law and order. The indifference has been combated by many attempts to enliven activities and worship. The charismatic movement has astonished and frightened, as well as enlivened interest. As in all religions, the more conservative elements have been more prosperous and grown, while the radical and liberal churches have declined in number. The reason is obvious, but disturbing. In times of change, when accepted standards of morality are disregarded, the conservative churches offer an attractive nostalgia. They present a confidence that has been lost, a defence of Victorian values, a so-called moral majority. David Edwards, in his book *The Futures of Christianity*, admits these nostalgic reasons, but eloquently describes also the positive strength of very conservative elements in the church:

> Conservative religion, precisely because it encourages an attitude of awestruck dependence on God . . . appeals to people in whom the religious sense is particularly strong. Sensing the presence of the eternal and all-holy reality in whom . . . are the depth of truth and the height of beauty, the combination . . . of sovereign power with compassionate love, such people do not wish to question or to argue. They 'take off their shoes'. They 'repent in dust and ashes'. They are content to adore and when they rise from their worship their wish is to obey the command which they have heard: the command to be pure with that purity.[2]

Although this can lead to an obscurantism and a sterile fundamentalism, it also produces individuals of great integrity and piety. They are the stuff that saints are made of, and their devotion to their tradition is absolute. In times of collapse, it has often been this conservative core that has preserved the church. They have guarded the mysteries.

THE FIRST PRIORITY IS NOT SURVIVAL

The church exists for the world. It is therefore in the world that we must find it.

Viraj Mendez, a political refugee from Sri Lanka, seeking and finding asylum in a church, discovered this in a dramatic way when fifty police surrounded the church and forced him to surrender his freedom. However much we may deplore this, we should not expect the 'church for the world' to be a safe place. In the general run of things it will be respected as a place of worship, but no sanctuary. Like the worker priests of France, it is now in the world and must take the 'slings and arrows of outrageous fortune' with the rest. Its life may be celebrated at the altar, but it is not lived there. It is lived where the poor are in need of good news, where prisoners cry out for release, where the blind long to see and where the oppressed long for liberation (Luke 4:18–19).

It is in the real world that the Year of Jubilee must be declared. And still, as in Nazareth, the people will gladly accept the wonderful teaching of that year, when all is forgiven, all debts are cancelled, all slaves are set free; but not all will want to hear that it is to happen now in their society. When the church proclaims the Nazareth sermon, it must of necessity be rejected by those in privileged positions. It cannot expect popularity, and indeed there is something wrong if all men speak well of the church. Dick Sheppard said many years ago that the church which really preached the gospel would soon be emptied. And Jesus gave the same warning to his disciples. The first priority of the church is not survival, but faithfulness to the gospel.

If the Spirit of God quickens the hearts of men and women so that they accept the message of the church as on the Day of Pentecost, we shall rejoice and celebrate, but we must not think that by our faithful representation of what we are compelled by our gospel to proclaim, or by any effort on our part, we should bring in a revival of Christianity in the land. Our task is not to be successful, but to serve those who are in need. We must do this regardless of success. The TV evangelists have shown us the dangers of making success our aim.

FINDING GOD IN THE MODERN WORLD

If our task is not to defend and enrich the citadel, but to go out into the modern world, we must go out unarmed and unprotected. We do not go to the world in confidence that, if in trouble, we can always run back to mother church, nor have we a magic sword to overcome all adversaries. We are disciples of one whose faithfulness led him to a cross, and he encourages us to expect no less. Of all the examples in recent decades of believers who have left the security of a formal church and found God in the modern world, the Roman Catholic Church has provided the clearest and most shattering.

'God in Fragments'

In 1979 Jacques Pohier, a Dominican priest, was banned by the Vatican from preaching, celebrating the Eucharist and teaching, because of a book which he had written two years before. In his book he had simply tried to follow out the teaching of Christ and interpret it in the modern world. The offensive passages were mostly to do with sexual relations between men and women.

Pohier had written from his deep Christian faith and the knowledge he had acquired by training in psychiatry. What the church took away from him was all he had. What is a Dominican who cannot preach, teach or celebrate the Eucharist? He remained a Dominican, and watched others do what he had been trained to do. He was broken by this experience. Then he decided to follow the insights which had taken him thus far, and go with them as far as he could go.

The book which had caused him to be banned, published in 1977, was entitled *Quand je dis Dieu* ('When I say God').[3] In the spring of 1979, the Vatican issued its condemnation and sentence. After the initial shock, which Pohier describes as 'decomposition', he began to write down his thoughts. He took three years to write *Dieu fractures*, a remarkable account of his pilgrimage in the world, which was later translated and published in English as *God in Fragments*.[4] The personal struggles and unexpected discoveries make this a compelling book. But more important than the personal odyssey is the main thesis that there are three areas of human life where the church has become so separated from the modern world as to be unintelligible. They are death, sexuality and guilt. If God is to be seen in these spheres of human life today, he must be a very different God from that of established Catholic tradition.

1 Death

In a long section of *God in Fragments*, in which Pohier examines the traditional attitude of a Catholic priest to death in the light of his experience with those who do not believe in the traditional Catholic faith and die with his comfort, he challenges many of our oft-repeated words. At the end of that section, he tells of Nadille, dying of cancer. She said to him, 'It is with your God that I want to die.'[5] His final paragraph shows what he has learnt as he let her go without faith in the resurrection of the dead:

> Do not say that I do not respect either death or God because I do not believe in the resurrection of the dead. Rather, help me to hear death, to hear the ebb and flow that it sets in motion. Do not make so much noise with your accusations, your objurations, your arguments. Nothing is important except the power to hear and understand. Help me to go to the other side. If you cannot help me or go with me there, do not forget me, remember that there are living beings on the other side. That they are human beings, living and mortal. Some of them want to live from God by Jesus Christ in his Spirit and be in communion with one another. Do not pursue us, do not reject us. Do not kill us, since death will kill you as it will kill us. In the name of God do not disdain to give us life and happiness, even if we are mortals as you are.[6]

That is a long way from the words that describe orthodox teaching about death and life after death, but it echoes the need of the world for the church. Pohier has gone out from the church and discovered that he has to serve the world with new sensitivity. Death was one of the spheres in which the church was thought to have a special role. Here it is clear that is it not fulfilling that role. Pohier's conclusions are confirmed by every empty and pious phrase at a funeral service.

2 Sexuality

With some hesitation, Pohier approached a subject which he considered as dangerous to discuss as death. His overall purpose he expressed as: to explore some of those other aspects [where] believers should spend time in order to be able to liberate God, to set him free, for him again to be able to introduce what he and a new humanity could achieve.[7] And he knew that the next aspect must be sexuality. Bonhoeffer too had listed as part of his stocktaking, Public morals – as shown by sexual behaviour.'[8]

There are few aspects of human life where traditional church teaching on 'public morals' are more apart from daily life than in sexuality. The celibate priesthood exaggerates this, the traumatic discussions over the ordination of women illustrate it, and the unacceptable link between faith and sexuality brought it to a climax in the experience of Jacques Pohier. It was in this field that he was condemned. When he wrote, he made use of the church fathers and the traditions of his church. But when his church sent him away from the celibate priesthood and into the world, he was no longer theoretical.

There have been changes in attitudes to sexuality which the church has refused to face. And in what Pohier calls 'the other side', *i.e.* the changed world, those changes have been unaided by the church. Neither have those changes ceased, and Pohier, like Bonhoeffer, pleads that the believers help the world to prepare for the future:

> The task of believers is not to decide on behalf of all human beings what sexuality must be on the other side, as if their status as believers gave them special insights . . .
>
> The gospel and tradition are not instruments for forecasting models for societies to come. They allow believers to help God make himself present to men and women in a given situation, to help the Spirit of Jesus Christ to introduce the 'God with us' among them and to ensure that a new form of human history can become a new form of the kingdom of God. That certainly does not mean that believers should absorb everything that comes into their world; faith is also judgement; criticism of the world.

However, even this function of criticism and judgement does not proceed *a priori* by inference from a model; it lies at the very heart of the development and the processes in which the gospel and tradition are light and company, warmth and power, joy and toil, searching and patience, support and rejection, courage to go forward but also deviations and set backs. That is why believers, even when they are theologians, do not primarily have the task of foreseeing what sexuality will be on the other side; their task is to go over there with the men and women who experience today's society in order to prepare tomorrow's society there and thus contribute towards shaping, constructing tomorrow's sexuality and making what contribution they can through the God of Jesus Christ and with him. As he said to us, 'Do not be afraid'.[9]

3 Guilt

The advent of psychoanalysis has given us a new perception of guilt. This makes it quite different from death and sexuality, because these have been with us for a long time! Guilt we now see as bound up with our view of God and certain practices of our faith. Guilt entangles believers in a slavery from which our view of God needs to be liberated.

Pohier asks three questions in relation to guilt and sin which arose out of his ministry during Holy Week some years before in a Breton village in France. Suddenly struck by the incongruity – he calls it 'out of place' – of much of the liturgy, which insisted upon confession of sin at what should surely be a party, or at least a celebration of the great world-saving act, he asked, 'Is sin as important as that?', or rather, 'Is sin important in that way?': in other words, 'Is that what matters to God?'[10] And throughout the liturgy of Maundy Thursday, Good Friday and Holy Saturday, he could not escape these questions:

> Why is sin accorded this privileged position, so that in fact it serves as the point of reference for the definition of man before God himself and that of Jesus Christ as Saviour? Why do we have to put sin first? Why do we make it the touchstone of all prayer, all spirituality, all theology?'[11]

Centuries before, although Pohier seems hardly to have noticed it, Job asked the same questions. While his friends called upon him to feel guilty and confess his sins, Job could not believe that his sins were all that important to God:

> What is man, that thou dost make so much of him,
> and that thou dost set thy mind upon him? . . .
> If I sin, what do I do to thee, thou watcher of men?
>
> (Job 7:17,20)

That is set down as a corrective, not a doctrine. Pohier is not saying, any more than Job was saying, that sin is unimportant. He merely questions the appropriate time and place for confession. We Christians live by grace, and we are not primarily under the tyranny of guilt. We live as forgiven people in the sunshine of God's love. As such, we rejoice in good and healthy things: 'whatever is true, whatever is honourable, whatever is just, whatever is pure, whatever is lovely, whatever is gracious, if there is any excellence, if there is anything worthy of praise, think about these things' (Philippians 4:8). With this atmosphere we go into the world, where thought and life are changing. We do not regret this change. We seize upon it with joy, for God is in it.

Our old categories will not do in this world which God is renewing – as active in the world, which he loves, as he is in the church, which he has called out. If instead of guarding our mysteries, we go out with that incredible openness which Jesus had, we shall need to help the world feel the ebb and flow of death and that God is in it. We shall learn from the changes in sexuality and help to form the new values with God in them. We shall listen to the new understanding of guilt, its dangerous corrosive effect upon human lives, and its proper place in a world which God has shot through with love.

Pohier says at the end of *God in Fragments* that looking at these changes has led him to a discovery about God which allows the human person to be free to live and love within the world which is never far from God. His discovery is that 'God is God, so God is not everything'.[12] There is a freedom in that discovery which in no way diminishes God. It allows us to worship God and retain our free place in his and our world. It is fragmentation, it reduces to fragments ideas and institutions of our faith and a number of our ideas about God, but it also and above all 'reduces to fragments the fetters under which we are bowed down, and allows us to stand upright – alive'.[13]

  It may not be easy to follow this brave and revolutionary Dominican, but for all his differences, he is moving in the direction that Bonhoeffer pointed towards, that place where we shall see the world changed and renewed by the utterance of the word of God: 'It will be a new language, perhaps quite non-religious, but liberating and redeeming . . .'[14]

NOTES

INTRODUCTION

1 Dietrich Bonhoeffer, *Letters and Papers from Prison: The Enlarged Edition*, ed. Eberhard Bethge (London: SCM Press, 1971), pp. 378–379.

2 *ibid.*, pp. 349–356.

3 *ibid.*, p. 352.

4 *ibid.*, p. 353.

5 *ibid.*, p. 354.

6 *ibid.*, p. 355.

7 *ibid.*, p. 378.

8 The English translation, *Letters and Papers from Prison*, was first published in 1953 by the SCM Press; the third, revised and enlarged, edition appeared in 1967, and the present enlarged edition was published in 1971.

9 John A. T. Robinson, *Honest to God* (London: SCM Press, 1963).

10 Bonhoeffer, *Letters and Papers from Prison*, pp. 380–383.

11 Eberhard Bethge, *Bonhoeffer: Exile and Martyr* (London: Collins, 1975), p. 141.

12 *ibid.*, pp. 137–154.

13 Bonhoeffer, *Letters and Papers from Prison*, pp. 370–371.

14 Bethge, *Bonhoeffer: Exile and Martyr*, p. 137.

15 Bonhoeffer, *Letters and Papers from Prison*, p. 359.

16 Bethge, 'B: Exile and Martyr', p. 142.

17 *ibid.* p. 327.

18 *ibid.*, p. 341.

19 *ibid.*, p. 380.

20 *ibid.*, p. 341.

21 *ibid.*, p. 381.

22 *ibid.*, pp. 299–300.

23 *ibid.*, p. 381.

24 Dietrich Bonhoeffer, *Ethics*, (London: SCM Press, 1955), pp. 46–50.
25 Bonhoeffer, *Letters and Papers from Prison*, p. 345.
26 *ibid.*, pp. 381–382.
27 Rabindranath Tagore, *Gitanjali* ('Song Offerings'), Macmillan, 1913, pp. 8–9.
28 Bethge, *Bonhoeffer: Exile and Martyr*, pp. 151–152.
29 Bonhoeffer, *Letters and Papers from Prison*, p. 382.
30 Bethge, *Bonhoeffer: Exile and Martyr*, p. 154.
31 Bonhoeffer, *Letters and Papers from Prison*, p. 383.

1 THE COMING OF AGE OF MANKIND

1 Sigmund Freud, *New Introductory Lectures on Psychoanalysis*, ed. Angela Richards, The Pelican Freud Library, vol. 2 (Harmondsworth: Penguin Books, 1973), pp. 203–204.
2 Dietrich Bonhoeffer, *Letters and Papers from Prison: The Enlarged Edition*, ed. Eberhard Bethge (London: SCM Press, 1971), pp. 359–360.
3 Jacques Monod, *Chance and Necessity* (London: Collins, 1972), p. 137.
4 *ibid.*, p. 167.
5 *The Phenomenon of Man* (Fontana, 1965), pp. 328–338.
6 Paul Davies, *The Cosmic Blueprint* (London: Heinemann, 1987), p. 203.
7 *e.g.* Stanley L. Jaki, *The Road of Science and the Ways to God* (Edinburgh: Scottish Academic Press; Chicago: University of Chicago Press, 1978).
8 Sergei Tarassenko, from a privately circulated paper.
9 Bonhoeffer, *Letters and Papers from Prison*, pp. 324–329.
10 *ibid.*, p. 326.
11 *ibid.*, p. 327.
12 Karl Barth, *The Epistle to the Romans*, tr. Edwyn C. Hoskyns (Oxford: Oxford University Press, 1933).
13 Bonhoeffer, *Letters and Papers from Prison*, p. 328.
14 *ibid.*, p. 329.
15 *ibid.*, p. 329.
16 *ibid.*, pp. 335–337.
17 *ibid.*, p. 337.
18 Daniel Jenkins, *Beyond Religion* (London: SCM Press, 1962), p. 75.

19 H. H. Kraemer, *The Theology of the Laity*, (Independent Press, 1958), p. 9.
20 H. H. Walz, *The Ecumenical Review* (April 1958), p. 282.
21 John MacKay, 'The Evils of Clericalism', *The Other Spanish Christ* (Macmillan, 1933).
22 Bonhoeffer, *Letters and Papers*, , p. 321.
23 Edward Norman, *Christianity and the World Order* (Oxford: Oxford University Press, 1979).
24 On many occasions in public addresses.

2 SPIRITUAL RESOURCES

1   *cf.* Dietrich Bonhoeffer, *Letters and Papers from Prison: The Enlarged Edition*, ed. Eberhard Bethge (London: SCM Press, 1971), p. 380.
2   Stafford Beer, *The Brain of the Firm* (The Professional Library, by arrangement with Allen Lane, The Penguin Press 1972).
3   *ibid.*, p. 217.
4   Bethge, *Dietrich Bonhoeffer*, pp. 235–6.
5   Bonhoeffer, *Letters and Papers from Prison*, p. 300.
6   *ibid.*, p. 300.
7   *ibid.*, p. 300.
8   *ibid.*, p. 298.
9   H. Richard Niebuhr, *The Responsible Self* (San Francisco: Harper & Row, 1963).
10 *ibid.*, p. 2.
11 Dietrich Bonhoeffer, *Ethics* (London: SCM Press, 1955), p. 236.
12 Niebuhr, *The Responsible Self*, p. 22.
13 *ibid.*, pp. 22–23.
14 *ibid.*, p. 65.
15 Bonhoeffer, *Letters and Papers from Prison*, p. 298.
16 Niebuhr, *The Responsible Self*, p. 86.
17 Bonhoeffer, *Ethics*, pp. 194–197.
18 *ibid.*, p. 195.
19 *ibid.*, p. 196.
20 Niebuhr, *The Responsible Self*, p. 177.
21 Bonhoeffer, *Letters and Papers from Prison*, p. 384.
22 *ibid.*, p. 385.
23 *ibid.*, p. 385.

24 Eberhard Bethge, *Dietrich Bonhoeffer: Theologian, Christian, Contemporary* (New York: Harper & Row; London: Collins, 1970).
25 *Kirchliche Zeitgeschichte* ('Contemporary Church History'), 1/1 (May 1988), p. 182.
26 *ibid.*, p. 182.
27 *ibid.*, pp. 151–186.
28 Full text in Franklin Littell, *The German Phoenix* (New York: Doubleday, 1960), pp. 189–190.
29 Bonhoeffer, *Ethics*, pp. 89–95.
30 *ibid.*, p. 93.
31 *ibid.*, pp. 89 and 95.
32 Keith W. Clements, *A Patriotism for Today* (Collins, 1984).
33 Bonhoeffer, *Ethics*, p. 94.

3 THE SUFFERING OF GOD IN A GODLESS WORLD

1 Dietrich Bonhoeffer, *Letters and Papers from Prison: The Enlarged Edition*, ed. Eberhard Bethge (London: SCM Press, 1971), pp. 348–349.
2 *ibid.*, p. 360.
3 *ibid.*, p. 361; but see the whole argument in the letter pp. 361–362.
4 Helen Waddell, *Peter Abelard* (London: The Reprint Society, 1950), pp. 269–270.
5 Bonhoeffer, *The Cost of Discipleship* (New York: Macmillan, 1963; London: SCM Press, 1959).
6 Bonhoeffer, *Letters and Papers from Prison*, p. 362.
7 *ibid.*, p. 362.
8 Gerd Theissen, *The Shadow of the Galilean: The Quest of the Historical Jesus in Narrative Form* (London: SCM Press, 1987), pp. 184–186.

4 THE CHURCH ON THE DEFENSIVE

1 See Klaus Scholder, *The Churches and the Third Reich: Volume One, Preliminary History and the Time of Illusions: 1918–1934* (London: SCM Press, 1987), p. 34.

2 *ibid.*, p. 35.
3 The *Evangelische Kirchenbund* was formed at the First Kirchentag, held in Dresden, 1–5 December 1919, leaving the independence of the provincial churches intact. The quote is from the minutes of that Kirchentag, published in 1920, which defined the purpose of the *Evangelische Kirchenbund*.
4 Quoted in Scholder, *The Churches and the Third Reich: Vol. 1, 1918–1934*, pp. 40–41.
5 Karl Barth, 'Biblical Questions, Insights, and Vistas' in *The Word of God and the Word of Man* (London: Hodder & Stoughton, 1957), pp. 62–63 (also quoted in Scholder, *The Churches and the Third Reich: Vol. 1, 1918–1934*, p. 42).
6 *ibid.*, p. 64.
7 *ibid.*, p. 67.
8 Dietrich Bonhoeffer, *Letters and Papers from Prison: The Enlarged Edition*, ed. Eberhard Bethge (London: SCM Press, 1971), p. 280.
9 *ibid.*, p. 280.
10 *ibid.*, p. 281; see also Bonhoeffer, *Ethics* (London: SCM Press, 1955), pp. 103–110.
11 *ibid.*, p. 281.
12 *ibid.*, p. 282.
13 *ibid.*, p. 286.
14 *ibid.*, pp. 317–318.
15 *ibid.*, p. 328.
16 *ibid.*, p. 329.
17 *ibid.*, p. 329.
18 *ibid.*, pp. 370–371.
19 *Kirchliche Zeitgeschichte* ('Contemporary Church History'), 1/1 (May 1988), pp. 172–173.
20 The version I quote below differs in several respects from that in Bonhoeffer's *Letters and Papers from Prison*, pp. 370–371, and is taken from Bonhoeffer's *Ethics*, p. xvii, where the title is 'Stations on the Way to Freedom' (rather than 'Stations on the Road to Freedom') and the first stanza is entitled 'Self-discipline' (rather than 'Discipline').
21 Scholder, *The Churches and the Third Reich: Vol. 1, 1918–1934*, pp. 40–41.
22 Bonhoeffer, *Letters and Papers from Prison*, p. 300.
23 Author's own translation.

PART 2 THE REAL MEANING OF CHRISTIAN FAITH: INTRODUCTION

1   John Bowden, *Jesus: The Unanswered Questions* (London: SCM Press, 1988), p. 1, quoting Bonhoeffer's letter of 30 April 1944 to Eberhard Bethge, from Dietrich Bonhoeffer, *Letters and Papers from Prison: The Enlarged Edition*, ed. Eberhard Bethge (London: SCM Press, 1971), p. 279.
2   Bowden, *Jesus: The Unanswered Questions*, p. xvii.

5   GOD AND WORLDLINESS

1   Dietrich Bonhoeffer, *Letters and Papers from Prison: The Enlarged Edition*, ed. Eberhard Bethge (London: SCM Press, 1971), pp. 41–47.
2   *ibid.*, pp. 41–42.
3   *ibid.*, p. 42.
4   *ibid.*, p. 46.
5   *ibid.*, p. 46.
6   Eberhard Bethge, *Bonhoeffer: Exile and Martyr* (London: Collins, 1975), p. 146.
7   Dietrich Bonhoeffer, *Ethics* (London: SCM Press, 1955), p. 171.
8   In most hymnbooks, *e.g. The English Hymnal*, no. 393; *The Baptist Hymnbook*, no. 257.
9   Bonhoeffer, *Ethics*, p. 178.
10 *ibid.*, p. 179.
11 *ibid.*, pp. 179–184.
12 Bonhoeffer, *Letters and Papers from Prison*, p. 300.
13 J. B. Phillips, *Letters to Young Churches* (London: Geoffrey Bles, 1947). Phillips later completed the whole New Testament, and it was published as *The New Testament in Modern English* (London: Geoffrey Bles, 1960).
14 Kenneth Taylor completed the whole Bible as *The Living Bible* (Wheaton, IL: Tyndale House Publishers, 1971). The following quotation from Colossians is from the British edition of *The Living Bible* (Eastbourne: Kingsway Publications, 1975).
15 Albert Schweitzer, *The Quest of the Historical Jesus* (1906 in German) (London: SCM Press, 1981).
16 T. R. Glover, *The Jesus of History* (London, 1917).
17 *The English Hymnal*, no. 407.

6 THE NON-RELIGIOUS INTERPRETATION OF BIBLICAL CONCEPTS

1 Nikos Kazantzakis, *The Last Temptation* (London: Faber & Faber 1975).
2 See also Edwin Robertson, *Breakthrough* (Belfast: Christian Journals Ltd, 1976), pp. 32–43.
3 The full text of Charles Birch's 1964 Camden Lectures was subsequently published as *God and Nature* (London, SCM Press, 1965).
4 Paul Davies, *The Cosmic Blueprint* (London: Heinemann, 1987).
5 Jacques Monod, *Chance and Necessity* (London: Collins, 1972), p. 167.
6 See also Charles Birch, *Confronting the Future* (Harmondsworth: Penguin Books, 1975).
7 Eberhard Bethge, *Bonhoeffer: Exile and Martyr* (London: Collins, 1975), pp. 137–138.
8 Henry Mottu, *Union Seminary Quarterly Review* Vol. XXV, No. 1 (1969), p. 11.
9 Philip Toynbee, *Part of a Journey* (London: Collins, 1981), pp. 21–22.
10 *ibid.*, pp. 22.
11 *ibid.*, pp. 20–21.
12 Quoted in John A. T. Robinson, *The Difference in Being a Christian Today* (London: Collins, 1972), p. 45.
13 John Bowden, *Jesus: The Unanswered Questions* (London: SCM Press, 1988), pp. 171–172.
14 Toynbee, *Part of a Journey*, p. 199.
15 *ibid.*, p. 200.
16 Alasdair MacIntyre (ed.), *Metaphysical Beliefs* (London: SCM Press, 1957).
17 Toynbee, *Part of a Journey*, p. 200.
18 Dietrich Bonhoeffer, *Ethics* (London: SCM Press, 1955), pp. 185–194.
19 *ibid.*, p. 188.
20 *ibid.*, p. 189.
21 *ibid.*, p. 189.
22 Bonhoeffer, *Letters and Papers from Prison*, pp. 324–329.
23 *ibid.*, p. 326.
24 *ibid.*, p. 371.
25 From J. B. Phillips, *Four Prophets* (London: Collins, 1967), pp. 76–77.

26 Bonhoeffer, *Ethics*, pp. 98–160.
27 *ibid.*, p. 98.
28 Sigmund Freud, *New Introductory Lectures on Psychoanalysis*, ed. Angela Richards, The Pelican Freud Library, vol. 2 (Harmondsworth: Penguin Books, 1973), p. 197.
29 Bonhoeffer, *Ethics*, p. 99.
30 *ibid.*, p. 99.
31 *ibid.*, p. 99.
32 *ibid.*, pp. 102–103.
33 *ibid.*, pp. 115–116.

7 RELIGIONLESS WORSHIP AND PRAYER

1 Dietrich Bonhoeffer, *Letters and Papers from Prison: The Enlarged Edition*, ed. Eberhard Bethge (London: SCM Press, 1971), pp. 278–282.
2 *ibid.*, p. 279.
3 *ibid.*, p. 280.
4 *ibid.*, p. 281.
5 Eberhard Bethge, *Dietrich Bonhoeffer: Theologian, Christian, Contemporary* (New York: Harper & Row; London: Collins, 1970), pp. 38–41; *cf.* Edwin Robertson, *The Shame and the Sacrifice* (London: Hodder & Stoughton, 1987), pp. 41–43.
6 Robertson, *The Shame and the Sacrifice*, pp. 190–193; Dietrich Bonhoeffer, *True Patriotism: Letters, Lectures and Notes 1939–1945*, ed. and introduced Edwin H. Robertson (London: Collins, 1973), pp. 72–76.
7 Robertson, *The Shame and the Sacrifice*, pp. 275–276.
8 Bonhoeffer, *Letters and Papers from Prison*, p. 300.
9 *ibid.*, pp. 369–370.
10 *ibid.*, p. 369.
11 For the phrase 'arcane discipline', see *ibid.*, p. 281; 'What is the place of worship and prayer in a religionless situation? Does the *secret discipline*, or alternatively the difference . . . between penultimate and ultimate, take on a new importance here?'
  Also, Bethge, *Bonhoeffer: Exile and Martyr*, p. 151.
12 *ibid.*, p. 361.
13 *ibid.*, p. 300.
14 *ibid.*, p. 297.
15 *ibid.*, p. 300.

16 Leon Joseph, Cardinal Suenens, *A New Pentecost?*, tr. Francis
   Martin (London: Darton, Longman & Todd, 1975), p. xii–xiii.
17 *ibid.*, pp. xii-xiii.
18 *ibid.*, p. 99.
19 see Edwin Robertson, *Corinthians One and Two*, The J. B.
   Phillips Commentaries (London: Collins, 1971), pp. 78–90.
20 Suenens, *A New Pentecost?*, p. 102.
21 See also Dietrich Bonhoeffer, *Meditating on the Word*, ed. and
   tr. David McI Gracie (Cambridge, MA., USA: Cowley
   Publications, 1986). Note especially the text of a meditation on
   Psalm 119, on pp. 101–145.
22 Edwin Robertson, *Chiara* (Belfast: Christian Journals Ltd,
   1978).
23 Edwin Robertson, *The Fire of Love: Igino Giordani*
   (London, New City, 1989).
24 Dietrich Bonhoeffer, *No Rusty Swords: Letters, Lectures and
   Notes 1928–1936*, ed. and introduced Edwin H. Robertson
   (London: Collins, 1970), p. 108.
25 Bonhoeffer, *Letters and Papers from Prison*, p. 300.

8   WHAT DO WE REALLY BELIEVE?

1 *Praise for Today* (London Psalms and Hymns Trust, 1974),
   no. 59.
2 R. S. Thomas (ed.), *The Penguin Book of Religious Verse*
   (Harmondsworth: Penguin Books, 1963), pp. 17–18.
3 John A. T. Robinson, *The Difference in Being a Christian
   Today* (London: Collins, 1972), p. 37.
4 The letters of 5 December and 15 December 1943, in Dietrich
   Bonhoeffer, *Letters and Papers from Prison: The Enlarged
   Edition*, ed. Eberhard Bethge (London: SCM Press, 1971),
   pp. 158 and 163 respectively.
5 Dietrich Bonhoeffer, *Ethics* (London: SCM Press, 1955),
   pp. 326–334.
6 *ibid.*, p. 328.
7 *ibid.*, p. 329.
8 *ibid.*, pp. 330–331.
9 *ibid.*, p. 331.
10 *ibid.*, p. 333.
11 Bonhoeffer, *Letters and Papers from Prison*, pp. 158–159, 163.
12 *ibid.*, p. 382; *cf.* p. 286.

13   Bonhoeffer, *Ethics*, p. 334 (*cf.* Bonhoeffer, *Letters and Papers from Prison*, pp. 158–159).
14   I have used here the translation from Bonhoeffer, *Letters and Papers from Prison*, pp. 158–159.
15   Paul Tillich, *The Shaking of the Foundations* (London: SCM Press, 1949; Harmondsworth: Penguin Books 1962).
16   Gibson Winter, *The Suburban Captivity of the Churches* (London: SCM Press, 1962).
17   Harvey Cox, *The Secular City* (London: SCM Press, 1965).
18   Eric James, *A Life of Bishop John A. T. Robinson: Scholar, Pastor, Prophet* (London: Collins, 1987), p. 113.
19   'On Being a Radical' was first published in *The Listener*, 21 February 1963, and subsequently appeared in Robinson's *Christian Freedom in a Permissive Society* (London: SCM Press, 1970). An extract from it is quoted in James, *A Life of Bishop John A. T. Robinson*, pp. 113–114.
20   James, *A Life of Bishop John A. T. Robinson*, p. 113.
21   Alec Vidler (ed.), *Soundings* (Cambridge: Cambridge University Press, 1962).
22   See. J. A. T. Robinson and D. L. Edwards (eds.), *The Honest to God Debate* (London: SCM Press, 1963).
23   Herbert Butterfield, *Christianity and History* (London: Collins, 1957), p. 189.
24   H. A. Williams, *The True Wilderness* (London: Constable, 1965).
25   Bonhoeffer, *Letters and Papers from Prison*, p. 382.
26   Dietrich Bonhoeffer, *No Rusty Swords: Letters, Lectures and Notes 1928–1936*, ed. and introduced Edwin H. Robertson (London: Collins, 1970), p. 67.
27   *ibid.*, p. 87.
28   Klaus Scholder, *The Churches and the Third Reich*, Vol. 1 (London: SCM Press, 1987), p. 457.
29   Eberhard Bethge, *Bonhoeffer: Exile and Martyr*, pp. 65–66.
30   Bonhoeffer, *No Rusty Swords*, pp. 286–287.
31   Bonhoeffer, *Letters and Papers from Prison*, p. 300.

PART 3   CONSEQUENCES FOR THE FUTURE OF THE CHURCH

INTRODUCTION

1 Eberhard Bethge, *Bonhoeffer: Exile and Martyr* (London: Collins, 1975).
2 Dietrich Bonhoeffer, *Letters and Papers from Prison: The Enlarged Edition*, ed. Eberhard Bethge (London: SCM Press, 1971), pp. 380–383.
3 *Kirchliche Zeitgeschichte* ('Contemporary Church History'), Part I, 1989.

9   CONSEQUENCES FOR THE FUTURE OF THE CHURCH

1 Ronald Gregor Smith, *The New Man* (London: SCM Press, 1956); see also Keith W. Clements, *The Theology of Ronald Gregor Smith* (Leiden: E. J. Brill, 1986).
2 *Faith in the City: The Report of the Archbishop of Canterbury's Commission on Urban Priority Areas* (London: Church House Publishing, 1985).
3 *Letters and Papers from Prison*, p. 349.
4 Antonio Pérez-Esclarín, *Atheism and Liberation* (London: SCM Press, 1978).
5 *ibid.*, p. 197.
6 *ibid.*, p. 199.
7 *Letters and Papers from Prison*, p. 382.
8 Dietrich Bonhoeffer, *Letters and Papers from Prison: The Enlarged Edition*, ed. Eberhard Bethge (London: SCM Press, 1971), pp. 347–348.
9 *ibid.*, pp. 349–356.
10 *ibid.*, p. 349.
11 *ibid.*, p. 352.
12 *ibid.*, p. 354.
13 *ibid.*, p. 355.
14 *ibid.*, p. 355.
15 Principally, Jürgen Moltmann, 'The Theology of Hope', (London: SCM Press), 1967.

16   Dorothee Sölle, *Choosing Life* (London: SCM Press, 1981).
17   *ibid.*, pp. 77–78.
18   Bonhoeffer, *Letters and Papers from Prison*, pp. 285–287.
19   *ibid.*, pp. 285–286.
20   *ibid.*, p. 286.
21   Stephen Neill, *Crises of Belief: The Christian Dialogue with Faith and No Faith* (London: Hodder & Stoughton, 1984).
22   *ibid.*, p. 284.
23   *ibid.*, p. 285.
24   *ibid.*, p. 285.
25   Based on Nikos Kazantzakis' novel *The Last Temptation* (London: Faber & Faber, 1975).
26   Salman Rushdie, *The Satanic Verses* (Harmondsworth: Penguin Books, 1988).
27   Neill, *Crises of Belief*, pp. 285 and 286 respectively.
28   G. F. Vicedom, *Church and People in New Guinea* (World Christian Books, 1961), pp. 16–17, cited in Neill, *Crises of Belief*, p. 287.
29   John Bowden, *Jesus: The Unanswered Questions* (London: SCM Press, 1988), p. 208.
30   *ibid.*, p. 208.
31   *ibid.*, p. 208.
32   *By Heart: A Lifetime Companion*, selected and ed. John Bowden (London: SCM Press, 1984).
33   Bonhoeffer, *Letters and Papers from Prison*, p. 383.
34   Eberhard Bethge, *Bonhoeffer: Exile and Martyr* (London: Collins, 1975), p. 154.
35   Isaac Watts, from the hymn, 'My dear Redeemer and my Lord'.
36   Neill, *Crises of Belief*, pp. 32–33.
37   *ibid.*, pp. 20–22.
38   Jacques Monod, *Chance and Necessity* (London: Collins, 1972).
39   Neill, *Crises of Belief*, p. 21.
40   C. S. Lewis, *The Problem of Pain* (1940) (London: Collins, 1957), p. 12.
41   Teilhard de Chardin has produced a library of books illustrating various aspects of this sense of purpose in our understanding of the world:
      eg. The Heart of Matter, Collins, London, 1978
          The Future of Man, Collins, London, 1964
          Christianity and Evolution, Collins, London, 1969.

This is in addition to the two fundamental works,
The Phenomenon of Man, Collins, London, paperback,
Fount/Fontana, 1959.
Milieu Divin, Collins, London, paperback, Fount/Fontana,
1960.

42 Paul Davies, *The Cosmic Blueprint* (London: Heinemann,
1987).
43 The documentation is to be found in, *The Worker Priests*
(French edition 1954), English translation by John Petrie
(London: Routledge & Kegan Paul, 1956). No complex is
named. It is a 'collective enterprise' of Worker Priests.
44 *ibid.*, pp. 13–14.
45 *ibid.*, p. 15.

EPILOGUE

1   John Foxe, contemporary accounts 16th century Protestant
martyrs.
2   David L. Edwards, *The Futures of Christianity* (London:
Hodder & Stoughton, 1987), p. 383.
3   Jacques Pohier, *Quand Je dis Dieu* (Paris: Les Editions du
Seuil, 1977).
4   Jacques Pohier, *God in Fragments*, tr. John Bowden (London:
SCM Press, 1985).
5   *ibid.*, p. 139.
6   *ibid.*, p. 139.
7   *ibid.*, p. 140.
8   Dietrich Bonhoeffer, *Letters and Papers from Prison: The
Enlarged Edition*, ed. Eberhard Bethge (London: SCM Press,
1971), p. 381.
9   Pohier, *God in Fragments*, pp. 198–199.
10 *ibid.*, p. 202.
11 *ibid.*, p. 215.
12 *ibid.*, pp. 261–314.
13 *ibid.*, p. 308.
14 Bonhoeffer, *Letters and Papers from Prison*, p. 300.

SELECT BIBLIOGRAPHY

Writings by Dietrich Bonhoeffer in English Translation
Sanctorum Communio: A Dogmatic Inquiry into the Sociology of the Church (London: Collins, 1963) – American title: *The Communion of Saints* (New York: Harper & Row, 1963)
Act and Being (New York: Harper & Row; London: Collins, 1962)
Creation and Fall: A Theological Interpretation of Genesis 1–3 (New York: Macmillan; London: SCM Press, 1959)
Christology (New York: Harper & Row; London: Collins, 1966; revised 1978) – American title: *Christ the Center*
Spiritual Care (Philadelphia: Fortress Press, 1985)
The Cost of Discipleship (New York: Macmillan, 1963; London: SCM Press, 1959)
Temptation (New York: Macmillan; London: SCM Press, 1955)
Life Together (New York: Harper & Row; London: SCM Press, 1954)
Psalms: The Prayer Book of the Bible (Minneapolis: Augsburg, 1970)
Ethics (New York: Macmillan; London: SCM Press, 1964)
I Loved This People (Richmond: John Knox Press, 1965)
Letters and Papers from Prison: The Enlarged Edition (New York: Macmillan; London: SCM Press, 1971)
Fiction from Prison: Gathering up the Past, ed. Renate and Eberhard Bethge, with Clifford Green (Philadelphia: Fortress Press, 1981)
Prayers from Prison, ed. J. C. Hampe (London: Collins, 1977)

English translations based on:
Dietrich Bonhoeffer Gesammelte Schriften ('Collected Works', Eberhard Bethge (ed.)) vols 1–6 (Munich: Chr. Kaiser Verlag, 1958–1974):
No Rusty Swords: Letters, Lectures and Notes, 1928–36, from the Collected Works of Dietrich Bonhoeffer, vol. 1, ed. and

introduced Edwin H. Robertson (New York: Harper & Row; London: Collins, 1965; revised John Bowden, 1970)

The Way to Freedom: Letters, Lectures and Notes, 1935–39, from the Collected Works of Dietrich Bonhoeffer, vol. 2, ed. and introduced Edwin H. Robertson (New York: Harper & Row; London: Collins, 1966)

True Patriotism: Letters, Lectures and Notes, 1939–45, from the Collected Works of Dietrich Bonhoeffer, vol. 3, ed. and introduced Edwin H. Robertson (New York: Harper & Row; London: Collins, 1973)

John de Gruchy, *Bonhoeffer and South Africa: Theology in Dialogue* (Grand Rapids: Wm B. Eerdmans, 1984)

Studies on Bonhoeffer's Life and/or Thought:

Eberhard Bethge, *Dietrich Bonhoeffer: Theologian, Christian, Contemporary* (London: Collins, 1970)

Eberhard Bethge, *Bonhoeffer: Exile and Martyr*, ed. and with an essay by John W. de Gruchy (London: Collins, 1975)

Eberhard Bethge, *Bonhoeffer: An Illustrated Introduction* (London: Collins, 1979)

Mary Bosanquet, *The Life and Death of Dietrich Bonhoeffer* (New York: Harper & Row, 1969; London: Hodder & Stoughton, 1968)

James H. Burtness, *Shaping the Future: Ethics of Dietrich Bonhoeffer* (Philadelphia: Fortress Press, 1985)

Keith W. Clements, *Patriotism for Today: Dialogue with Dietrich Bonhoeffer* (Bristol: Bristol Baptist College, 1984)

Oho Dudzus (ed.), *Bonhoeffer for a New Generation* (London: SCM Press, 1986)

André Dumas, *Dietrich Bonhoeffer: Theologian of Reality* (New York: Macmillan, 1971)

Ernst Feil, *Theology of Dietrich Bonhoeffer* (Philadelphia: Fortress Press, 1985)

John D. Godsey, *The Theology of Dietrich Bonhoeffer* (Philadelphia: Westminster Press; London: SCM Press, 1960)

William B. Gould, *The Worldly Christian: Bonhoeffer and Discipleship* (Philadelphia: Fortress Press, 1967)

John de Gruchy (ed.), *Dietrich Bonhoeffer: Witness to Jesus Christ*, The Making of Modern Theology 4 (London: Collins, 1987)

Kenneth Hamilton, *Life in One's Stride: A Short Study in Dietrich Bonhoeffer* (Grand Rapids: Wm B. Eerdmans, 1968)

William Kuhns, *In Pursuit of Dietrich Bonhoeffer* (Dayton: Pflaum Press, 1967; London: Burns & Oates, 1968)

Rene Marle, *Bonhoeffer: The Man and His Work* (New York: Newman Press, 1968)

Martin E. Marty, *The Place of Bonhoeffer: Problems and Possibilities in His Thought* (London: Greenwood Press, 1981)

Jürgen Moltmann and Jürgen Weissbach, *Two Studies in the Theology of Bonhoeffer* (New York: Scribners, 1967)

John A. Phillips, *The Form of Christ in the World: A Study of Bonhoeffer's Christology* (London: Collins, 1967) – American title: *Christ for Us in the Theology of Dietrich Bonhoeffer* (New York: Harper & Row, 1967)

Benjamin A. Reist, *The Promise of Bonhoeffer* (Philadelphia: Lippincott, 1969)

Edwin Robertson, *Dietrich Bonhoeffer* (Richmond: John Knox Press; London: Carey Kingsgate Press, 1966)

Edwin Robertson, *The Shame and the Sacrifice: The Life and Teaching of Dietrich Bonhoeffer* (London: Hodder & Stoughton, 1987)

Ronald Gregor Smith (ed.), *World Come of Age* (Philadelphia: Fortress Press; London: Collins, 1967)

Peter Vorkink (ed.), *Bonhoeffer in a World Come of Age* (Philadelphia: Fortress Press, 1968)

J. W. Woelfel, *Bonhoeffer's Theology: Classical and Revolutionary* (Nashville: Abingdon Press, 1970)

Wolf-Dieter Zimmermann and Ronald Gregor Smith (eds), *I Knew Dietrich Bonhoeffer: Reminiscences by his Friends* (New York: Harper & Row; London: Collins, 1966)

Other Works Referred to in the Text

The following is a list of those works not already listed above which have been referred to in the text and notes of *Bonhoeffer's Heritage*:

The Archbishop of Canterbury's Commission on Urban Priority Areas, *Faith in the City* (London: Church House Publishing, 1985)

Karl Barth, *The Epistle to the Romans*, tr. Edwyn C. Hoskyns (Oxford: Oxford University Press, 1933)

Karl Barth, 'Biblical Questions, Insights, and Vistas' in *The Word of God and the Word of Man* (London: Hodder & Stoughton, 1957)

Stafford Beer, *The Brain of the Firm* (London: The Professional Library, 1972)

Charles Birch, *God and Nature* (London, SCM Press, 1965)

Charles Birch, *Confronting the Future* (Harmondsworth: Penguin Books, 1975)

John Bowden (ed.), *By Heart: A Lifetime Companion* (London: SCM Press, 1984)

John Bowden, *Jesus: The Unanswered Questions* (London: SCM Press, 1988)

Herbert Butterfield, *Christianity and History* (London: Collins, 1957)

Teilhard de Chardin, see Notes

Keith W. Clements, *The Theology of Ronald Gregor Smith* (Leiden: E. J. Brill, 1986)

Harvey Cox, *The Secular City* (London: SCM Press, 1965)

Paul Davies, *The Cosmic Blueprint* (London: Heinemann, 1987)

David L. Edwards, *The Futures of Christianity* (London: Hodder & Stoughton, 1987)

Sigmund Freud, *New Introductory Lectures on Psychoanalysis*, ed. Angela Richards, The Pelican Freud Library, vol. 2 (Harmondsworth: Penguin Books, 1973)

T. R. Glover, *The Jesus of History* (London, 1917)

Stanley L. Jaki, *The Road of Science and the Ways to God* (Edinburgh: Scottish Academic Press; Chicago: University of Chicago Press, 1978)

Eric James, *A Life of Bishop John A. T. Robinson: Scholar, Pastor, Prophet* (London: Collins, 1987)

Daniel Jenkins, *Beyond Religion* (London: SCM Press, 1962)

Nikos Kazantzakis, *The Last Temptation* (London: Faber & Faber 1975)

H. H. Kraemer, *The Theology of the Laity* (London, 1958)

C. S. Lewis, *The Problem of Pain* (1940) (London: Collins, 1957)

Franklin Littell, *The German Phoenix* (New York: Doubleday, 1960)

Alasdair MacIntyre (ed.), *Metaphysical Beliefs* (London: SCM Press, 1957)

John MacKay, *The Other Spanish Christ* (New York: Macmillan, 1933)

Jacques Monod, *Chance and Necessity* (London: Collins, 1972)

Henry Mottu, New York, *Union Seminary Quarterly Review* Vol. XXV, No. 1, pp. 1–18, (1969)

Stephen Neill, *Crises of Belief: The Christian Dialogue with Faith and No Faith* (London: Hodder & Stoughton, 1984)

H. Richard Niebuhr, *The Responsible Self* (San Francisco: Harper & Row, 1963)

Edward Norman, *Christianity and the World Order* (Oxford: Oxford University Press, 1979)

Antonio Pérez-Esclarín, *Atheism and Liberation* (London: SCM Press, 1978)

J. B. Phillips, *Letters to Young Churches* (London: Geoffrey Bles, 1947)

J. B. Phillips, *The New Testament in Modern English* (London: Geoffrey Bles, 1960)

J. B. Phillips, *Four Prophets* (London: Collins, 1967)

Jacques Pohier, *Quand Je dis Dieu* (Paris: Les Editions du Seuil, 1977)

Jacques Pohier, *God in Fragments*, tr. John Bowden (London: SCM Press, 1985)

Edwin Robertson, *Breakthrough* (Belfast: Christian Journals Ltd, 1976)

Edwin Robertson, *Corinthians One and Two*, The J. B. Phillips Commentaries (London: Collins, 1971)

Edwin Robertson, *Chiara* (Belfast: Christian Journals Ltd, 1978)

Edwin Robertson, *The Fire of Love: Igino Giordani* (London: New City, 1989)

John A. T. Robinson, *Honest to God* (London: SCM Press, 1963)

John A. T. Robinson, *The Difference in Being a Christian Today* (London: Collins, 1972)

J. A. T. Robinson and D. L. Edwards (eds), *The Honest to God Debate* (London: SCM Press, 1963)

J. A. T. Robinson, *Christian Freedom in a Permissive Society* (London: SCM Press, 1970)

John A. T. Robinson, *The Difference in Being a Christian Today* (London: Collins, 1972)

Salman Rushdie, *The Satanic Verses* (Harmondsworth: Penguin Books, 1988)

Klaus Scholder, *The Churches and the Third Reich: Volume One, Preliminary History and the Time of Illusions: 1918–1934* (London: SCM Press, 1987)

Albert Schweitzer, *The Quest of the Historical Jesus* (London: SCM Press, 1981), first published in German in 1906

Ronald Gregor Smith, *The New Man* (London: SCM Press, 1956)

Dorothee Sölle, *Choosing Life* (London: SCM Press, 1981)

Leon Joseph, Cardinal Suenens, *A New Pentecost?*, tr. Francis Martin (London: Collins, 1977)

Kenneth Taylor, *The Living Bible* (Wheaton, IL: Tyndale House Publishers, 1971; Eastbourne: Kingsway Publications, 1975)

Gerd Theissen, *The Shadow of the Galilean: The Quest of the Historical Jesus in Narrative Form* (London: SCM Press, 1987)

R. S. Thomas (ed.), *The Penguin Book of Religious Verse* (Harmondsworth: Penguin Books, 1963)

Paul Tillich, *The Shaking of the Foundations* (London: SCM Press, 1949; Harmondsworth: Penguin Books 1962)

Philip Toynbee, *Part of a Journey* (London: Collins, 1981)

G. F. Vicedom, *Church and People in New Guinea* (London: World Christian Books, 1961)

Alec Vidler (ed.), *Soundings* (Cambridge: Cambridge University Press, 1962)

H. A. Williams, *The True Wilderness* (London: Constable, 1965)

Gibson Winter, *The Suburban Captivity of the Churches* (London: SCM Press, 1962)

The Worker Priests (French edition 1954), tr. John Petrie (London: Routledge & Kegan Paul, 1956)

INDEX

226 BONHOEFFER'S HERITAGE